LIGHT RA

& Guided Transit

A guide to
What,
Where,
Why, When
and How in
the new
forms of
urban
transport.

M. F. Powell.

Foreword

By Neil Kinnock, European Commissioner for Transport.

Good public transport matters. It can offer a better environment, a stronger economy and greater freedom of mobility for everyone - and by combating conjestion in urban areas and isolation in rural areas, it can make a direct contribution to the vitality of the whole society.

National and local authorities, the transport industry and transport users are all committed to creating public transport systems that people happily choose to use. The European Union is working to support them. We are helping transport planners and operators to exchange good ideas, compare their performance with others' and research new techniques - as well as reviewing legal frameworks to promote the development of public transport.

In all this, light rail has great potential.

Of course, it will never be the answer to every transport need - nothing is. But it really can come into its own in densely populated urban areas, or where there are high traffic flows from suburbs to city centres, by providing a very cost-effective way of serving existing markets and creating new ones. Light rail's high visibility, attractive public image, accessibility to people with mobility impairments, and the use of techniques like segregated lines and priority signalling at junctions are all assets in the effort to encourage the public to make greater use of public transport.

For all these reasons, I welcome the light rail renaissance in Europe. I am old enough to remember the last tram services in the UK - and delighted to be part of the movement to create their modern successors.

Neil Kinnock, Brussels, July 1997

© Michael F. Powell 1997   Illustrations: author's own photographs.
ISBN 1 897 887 03 5

Produced by Natula Publications
5 St Margaret's Avenue, Christchurch, Dorset BH23 1JD
British Library Cataloguing - in - Publication Data.
A catalogue record for this book is available from the British Library.

Acknowledgments.

I am indebted to the following organisations for generously supplying information on their products and services and, in many cases, for checking and advising on the draft. Whilst their support has been invaluable any errors or omissions remain my own:

ABB; Adtranz; AMT (Genova); AEG Westinghouse Transportation Systems Inc.; Ansaldo Trasporti; Ove Arup and Partners; Association of Metropolitan Authorities; ATAC (Rome); ATAN (Naples); ATM (Milan); Babcock Rail Ltd.; Blackpool Transport; Bombardier Transportation; Brecknell Willis &Co. Ltd.; Breda Costruzioni Ferroviarie Spa; Brighton Borough Council; BVB (Basle); Centro; Chapman Seating Ltd.; Communaute Urbaine de Lille; Companhia Carris de Ferro de Lisboa SA.; Deutsch Ltd.; Docklands Light Railway; Dopravni podnik hl. m. Prahy AS.; Edilon BV; Firema Trasporti Spa; GEC Alsthom; Greater Nottingham Rapid Transit Ltd.; Grwp Aberconwy; Hampshire County Council; HKL (Helsinki); HTM (Hague); HVV (Heidelberg); Intamin AG.; John Mowlem Construction plc; Kennedy Henderson Ltd.; Krone Rew; London Docklands Development Corporation; London Underground Ltd.; Manchester Metrolink; Metropolitan Transportation Authority (Los Angeles); Municipal Mass Transport Repair Shops (Prague); MVA; National Tramway Museum; Network Tram Engineering Services; Port Authority of Allegheny County; Regional Transit Authority (Seattle); RET (Rotterdam); San Diego Trolley Inc; San Fransisco Municipal Railway; Seaton and District Electric Tramway; Siemens AG.; SL (Stockholm); SMART (Detroit); SMC Pneumatics (UK) Ltd.; Southeastern Pennsylvania Transportation Authority; Spie Eurotrans; Stadtwerke Frankfurt am Main; STAS (St. Etienne); STIB (Brussels); Strathclyde PTE; SVB (Bern); SWM (Munich); South Yorkshire Supertram; TAG (Grenoble); TAN (Nantes); TCAR (Roeun); Thorn Transit Systems International; Tickford Rail Ltd.; TNB (Barcelona); Transcet SA.; Transport & General Workers Union; Transport 2000; The Transportation Group Inc.; Trasporti Torinesi; Tri-Met; Tyne and Wear PTE: USTRA (Hannover); VAG (Freiburg I B); VBZ (Zurich); Von Roll Transport Systems Ltd.; Washington State Department of Transportation; Westway Project (Bristol); West Yorkshire PTE; W. S. Atkins; Wiener Linien.

Every effort has been made to ascertain the copyright on certain illustrations. I apologise for any accidental infringement which may inadvertantly have occurred.

In addition I am very grateful to Margaret, Alex and Bryony (respectively my wife and children) for their typing, navigation, general calming skills and patience.

M.F. Powell
February 1997.

Contents.

Modern tramway and light rail systems may be incorporated into existing urban environments, even pedestrianised areas. In this case the city has changed around the tramway. Geneva in the rain.

LIGHT RAIL AND GUIDED TRANSIT.

Introduction.

Pollution, congestion, noise, physical hazards and increasing dereliction are facts of urban life at the end of the Twentieth century. They have been noted since the end of the Second World War and reports on their effects, dangers and solution (or partial reduction) have appeared more or less regularly since the 1960s. No concerted action has taken place on any such recommendations.

A number of piecemeal attempts have been made here and there but, in the absence of any overall policy, the town-dweller has been left to it, urged with increasing stridency to cut back on car use, set up neighbourhood watches, report polluters but provided with no adequate alternatives to what are recognised as the situation's causes. That would, of course, cost money and raise politically unacceptable objections.

To help with the required trend towards a useable, integrated transport solution bus services have been de-regulated (resulting in a 25% decline in ridership since its inception), railways are being privatised, having already lost their unity as a service, and public money is becoming increasingly unavailable for transport infrastructure with the exception of roads. Motorists will soon be required to pay to enter town centres or to use motorways for which they have already paid in taxes. No alternatives are suggested and those which already exist are being reduced in efficiency whilst increasing in cost.

Minibus City! In Exeter (UK) and elsewhere intensive minibus services attempt to solve the problems of congestion.

Road pricing is already practised at some unavoidable traffic nodes. There are plans to extend the principle to both motorways and town centres. Toll booths, Itchen Bridge, Southampton (UK).

With sufficient will there are solutions to many of the difficulties described above. These are neither imaginary nor cripplingly expensive. They are not unusable extravaganzas. There are a range of options all of which already exist elsewhere. These have been proved not only to work but to positively enhance the environment and provide the persuasion needed to get travellers to try alternatives to their cars.

Light rail is a term which has begun to appear with increasing frequency in the various news and current affairs media. It is usually associated with efforts to provide an alternative public transport system in towns and cities whose roads are already fully occupied.

This concept is often referred to in a manner which gives it the appearance of either a panacea to all modern, urban ills or an expensive, experimental, potential white elephant whose carcase will block further progress. Rarely is it mentioned as one of a range of options and it is not often explained.

There is a wealth of both historical and contemporary literature on the subject of railways. Magazines on public road transport enjoy a regular place on the newsagents' shelves. A substantial and expanding collection of publications covers many aspects of the history of tramways. Relatively little exists concerning modern tramways, light rail or guided transport systems and this tends to assume that it is updating existing knowledge.

The object of this book is to explain what modern tramways, light rail and guided transport systems

In Europe traffic congestion in town centres is reduced by offering a practical alternative. Handbill for park and ride, Freiburg (Germany).

Street running in an historic environment. Grenoble's low-floor cars have provided a pattern for other cities in France.

are, their purpose, range, context, technology and practice. It is not intended to be a technical manual, although technical aspects are considered, neither is it an historical survey, although development is not ignored.

It is aimed at providing an accessible source of information on a subject of increasing interest and importance for anyone who would like to know more.

A range of differing types of guided transport has developed to answer the needs of particular situations (such as at airports and tourist attractions) or in response to the apparently higher initial cost of steel-tracked systems. Ideally, they should be seen as major parts of the spectrum of modes of transport available to construct an overall, integrated transport system.

Trams, light rail and funiculars are not objects from a past era. Monorails, people-movers and guided transport systems are not subjects only for science fiction. They represent, in their present and developing forms, practical, efficient, user-friendly, quiet and relatively pollution-free solutions to many of the problems besetting transport in urban (and other) environments.

At the time of writing, the United Kingdom possesses five urban tramway and light rail systems, eight 'heritage' systems, eleven museums with operating tramways of various types, three pier tramways, seven transit systems within shopping centres, airports and other sites which come within a broad definition of 'mass transit' (including three in theme parks and other attractions) plus thirteen urban or

Marseilles' (France) single tram route has its inbound terminus in an underground station shared with the metro.

The urban funicular at Le Havre (France) links the upper and lower parts of the town via a tunnel. The cars have pneumatic tyres.

Automated 'people mover', again with pneumatic tyres, operating between the terminals at Gatwick Airport (West Sussex).

seaside funiculars - a total of forty-seven centres with more planned.

These exclude steam-hauled, narrow and standard gauge, preserved railways which are defined as 'light railways'.

In spite of this, a recent, informal survey (1994) indicated the level of awareness and understanding of such systems. It was conducted amongst sixth-form school students studying 'technology' and first year under-graduates who were reading environmentally based subjects.

Two-thirds of the respondents had never before heard the term 'light rail'. Only just over a quarter indicated any clear idea of what types of systems were involved whilst less than a fifth had any idea how systems could be included in existing urban environments. Fewer than one in twenty understood which kinds of routes might be served. (Four times as many thought it was for inter-city use.) Of the third who had heard the term, nearly all could name two places in the UK served by such systems although only one in twelve knew (or guessed) how many such systems there were in the country. Of those who claimed to have seen or travelled on light rail systems, more than three out of ten named places where such they do not exist. The survey was informal and intended to provide no more than the roughest indication, but these returns were from groups who might reasonably be expected to be more aware than most of such trends.

In the belief that such systems will become more important as concern over road usage, pollution

Monorails are rare as transit systems. This AEG straddle system is at Merry Hill (West Midlands).

The preservation movement at its pinnacle is represented by the National Tramway Museum at Crich (Derbyshire).

The principal sites within the North of England Open Air Museum at Beamish are served by tram.

and the quality of urban life increases, and, in the light of developing trends towards expectations of awareness and 'judgment by opinion poll', the following sections may provide a simple, introductory outline.

Modern light rail in the UK. Sheffield car crossing the bowstring bridge as it approaches Fitzalan Sq. in the city centre. The bridge is shared with pedestrians.

The Castle Hill funicular at Bridgenorth (Shropshire) has linked Upper and Lower Towns for over a century.

The tramway along Hythe Pier (Hampshire) operates in conjunction with the Southampton ferries.

The PCC car represented a major step forward in
technology and design when it was introduced during the 1930s. Later cars of this type are still operational. Ghent, Belgium.

LIGHT RAIL AND GUIDED TRANSIT.

Section 1.

Why and How - The Background.

Until the beginning of the so-called Industrial Revolution, around two-hundred and fifty years ago, urban settlements, with few exceptions, tended to be relatively small places. The vast majority of people lived on the land - country dwellers sleeping close to the fields in which they spent the majority of their working lives.

The first factories were also in the countryside. Their machinery was powered by the flow of water and, as a consequence, they were built by fast-flowing streams. Their machinery was activated by the same force which, for centuries, had ground corn and, as industrial centres, their sites were often extremely inconvenient.

Cityscape with tram approaching the Hauptbahnhof, Basle (Switzerland). Private motor traffic is reduced as a result of intensive public transport services.

In theory the introduction of steam power meant that factories could be constructed wherever they were required, such as near the ports or the markets for their products. In practice this only worked if their heat source, initially charcoal later coal, could be supplied conveniently. Steam-powered factories tended to be built in the coalfields where there were often iron deposits as well.

In the early stages, as it developed, the Industrial Revolution called for increasing numbers of workers. They were supplied from the countryside as enclosure of the old, open fields and concurrent improvements in agriculture freed them. The problem for the expanding industrial towns of the late Eighteenth and early Nineteenth

Many of Turin's (Italy) tram routes converge on the Porta Nuova station, as they did in the 1920s, providing access from the railway terminus to all parts of the city.

centuries was not acquiring a workforce but housing it.

Factory workers were often expected, in the early phase, to labour for up to sixteen hours each day. They had, therefore, to live very close to the factory itself. There was neither sufficient time nor energy to spend hours on foot going to and from work. The difficulty was solved by producing housing, as intensively arranged and as close to the factory gates as possible. Often houses, and even rooms, were let to two or more families who 'hot-bunked' as the shifts rotated.

This solution, the last vestiges of which lasted in some places until the last quarter of the Twentieth century, produced problems of its own. These were principally sanitation and disease. The Great Plague of the Seventeenth century paled into insignificance against the depredations of cholera and typhoid. Eventually, the technology of the industrial revolution itself was harnessed, in the form of steam pumps for sewage works and factories producing vitreous piping, to provide a solution. But the great problem remained. The workforce had to live within walking distance of its place of work.

The sudden development of large centres of population, and the need to sell the products that were produced within them, required a wholly new approach to transport. The concept of public transport was in its infancy when the revolution began. Towns were linked by stagecoaches, the best of which were those operated on behalf of the Royal Mail, operating along the new turnpikes, an early result of the need to travel quickly on business.

In addition to long distance links (top), railways also provide services within larger urban areas. South-eastern England possesses an extensive third-rail, electric network (above) centred on London. Elsewhere diesel multiple units are extensively used for both suburban and what used to be termed 'branch line' services (below).

By the end of the Eighteenth century a large proportion of industrial material and products were being carried by canal craft but these, like the stagecoaches, were soon in competition with the earliest railways. Railways could carry both freight and passengers with equal facility. All these modes, though, were principally employed over long distances. They did not immediately meet the urban transport need.

During the 1820s experiments were tried in Paris and London with 'omnibuses' (basically stagecoaches which could be used without booking in advance). With the exception of the Royal Mail coaches, upon which passengers were secondary to the mail, fares often varied with the number of passengers. The 'omnibus' had a fixed system, regardless of load. Even so fares were expensive and the service inadequate for mass transport purposes. London remained largely a close-knit group of 'villages' each with its own population, workforce and recognised limits.

By the 1840s railways were common and increasing all the time. They enabled people who so wished to live outside the cities and commute to work. They effectively created the suburbs but did not solve the inner cities' problems. Although railways were obliged by law to operate workmen's trains they made no great inroads into reducing urban crowding. The inefficiency of owning rolling-stock which was used only at peak times was soon realised. This problem has never been resolved.

So, the vast majority of workers in urban areas continued to live as close to their employment as possible.

During the Nineteenth century thousands of miles of railways were built throughout Europe. Linking together cities, towns and remote villages. The trackbed of the Wooton Tramway was once part of the Metropolitan Railway, a major London Suburban Service provider.

During the last three decades main lines (principally those considered uneconomic) have been closed. The line across Tregaron Moor in mid-Wales once linked S.W. Wales with northern England.

Like many such upheavals, the Industrial Revolution happened in a number of stages. The first provided the workforce and began the trend of urban growth. The second, the 'steam revolution', created a situation which it could not solve. The third stage, the development and use of electric power, at last provided a means of solution.

It is generally true that very few inventions are the result of a sudden flash of inspired light. Most are the result of painstaking research to provide a solution to a particular question. The steam railway itself is a combination of metal technology in the fields of track, boilers, cylinder design, vehicle fabrication and so on. In turn some of these developed from earlier technologies. Timber track for mining trucks had existed since the Fifteenth century and waggons were guided by grooves in the dockside at Ostia in Roman times. Flanges were originally on the track, not the wheel. High pressure boilers and accurate cylinders required the development of machinery to make them. Then, of course, those who can invest in the results have to be convinced that it will pay to do so. The time has to be right and the need apparent.

None of this occurs in isolation. So with the application of electricity to transport. The idea of tracked vehicles in the street was introduced into Britain in 1860 by an American entrepreneur, George Train. His track stood proud of the road surface and was not convenient to other road users. His horse-drawn vehicles could, though, haul over twice the load per animal compared with conventional wheeled road vehicles.

Interlaced tram track preserved in Rugby Road, Portsmouth (UK). Portsmouth possessed an extensive urban network together with an 'interurban' service to Horndean. Both closed prior to the Second World War but their routes remain largely duplicated by buses.

Once the track design had been resolved by introducing the concept of a groove, horse-trams appeared in a number of cities during the 1870s. Within a very short period specially designed steam locomotives had been introduced and such systems as cable-haulage were being tried.

During the 1880s electricity was applied to the concept. It had required the development of suitable motors and means of collecting the current but once it was shown to work the electric tram became the vehicle which enabled the workforce, for the first time, to live beyond walking range of the factories. The idea of industrial, residential and business zones now became practical. This did not occur at a stroke and is still developing. The worst excesses of the overcrowding resulting from industrialisation have been ameliorated by this means of transport in the United Kingdom, United States and Europe.

The earliest electric railway in the UK was the Volk's Railway, Brighton.

Like earlier systems, trams eventually fell to newer developments. It has taken many years for it to become apparent that these replacements, in terms of moving large numbers of people over well-used routes, cheaply, were not an improvement. Fortunately the technology continued to be developed elsewhere and the tram, or modes which have grown from that concept, is once again seen as a solution to some of the results of its replacements.

Whilst many European countries retained their tramway systems this was not so in the United Kingdom or the Americas. In both those areas, together with European countries which had allowed them to be replaced and some places

End of the line for the Ryde Pier (Isle Of Wight) tramway which, for more than a century, carried passengers to and from the steamers to the mainland.

which never used 'first-generation' systems, light-rail is being revived. Modern systems may appear to bear little resemblance to their forebears but the concept - the basic idea - is the same. The provision of fast, relatively inexpensive transport which can be fitted into existing urban environments and which is, due to the power station being elsewhere, pollution-free at the point of use.

Nearly two generations have grown up since the first generation of trams ceased to be a common sight. The new, technologically-advanced systems are seeking to provide a whole range of practical transport solutions. How they developed, how they work, what they do and how they fit in are outlined below.

Piazza del Duomo, Milan (Italy) around the turn of the century (above). Trams provided transport to, but did not detract from its splendour. Some thirty years later trams continued to carry a majority of the cities' travellers from the crowded inner suburbs (Corso Buenos Ayres, below). Milan still possesses an extensive tramway system.

The Urban Environment - A Legacy of the Immediate Past.

Light rail offers a highly-developed, high quality passenger transport system ideal for a wide range of defined corridors in urban areas and with applications for rural routes.

One of the hallmarks of the Twentieth Century has been the increase in urbanisation and the growth of cities. With many of the earlier problems such as overcrowding and insanitary conditions having been overcome, at least amongst developed nations, others have arisen in their stead. A major one is that of urban transportation.

So successful has been the marketing of the private car, together with the concept of permanently accessible, personal mobility that, in many parts of the world, it is a possession of the majority and an expectation of the remainder. Even

where road construction and control technology have approximately kept up with traffic growth, the congestion, pollution and physical dangers created by the presence of large numbers of vehicles in the finite space within cities, remains a largely unaddressed problem.

A commuter by car spends a part of each journey either stationary or travelling slowly. This represents the equivalent of many working lives wasted every day but cannot be fully computed. Calculations of cost can be made, however, for those who drive for a living; for example freight, emergency services, sales and maintenance teams, public transport and so on. The total resource costs of car and infrastructure construction may also be calculated.

The traditional answer to traffic congestion is to provide more road space, dual carriageways. Within urban areas one-way systems and flyover separation schemes are popular means of endeavouring to ensure continued traffic flow. The proportion of land required for road improvement depends on a number of factors. Amongst these the size of the town is possibly the most influential. Relatively small towns may be adequately served by existing, single carriageway roads. As the volume of traffic grows so these need to become multi-lane, then dualised, then duplicated. In large towns there is also a need to provide for traffic flow between centres within the urban area, as opposed to bringing traffic in from outside.

Additional problems arise from seasonal changes and tidal flows at different times of day. Once in town, vehicles must be parked somewhere. The average car requires about eleven square metres of space. A large proportion of

An earlier generation of tram in Ostend, on the Belgian coastal tramway. Within the built-up areas much of the track is on-street. The service provides urban, rural and interurban functions.

The European atmosphere of the Rue des Soeurs in Alexandria (Egypt), is partly a result of the Belgian built and owned tramway system.

urban ground area is occupied by roads and parking areas.

The success of such schemes as exist for reducing congestion may be measured by the fact that in London, for example, traffic speeds are lower now than they were fifty years ago. There is serious concern over the occurrence of 'gridlock', where opposing traffic flows block each other to the extent that nothing can move.

A prognosis of increased motoring, access and parking charges is that many current car commuters will elect to use alternative means of transport. This will, it is argued, result in less traffic, reduced congestion and other benefits. It assumes that suitable alternatives exist. Whilst commuters may have a choice of transport modes in town, this may be severely restricted at the other end of their journeys. This may be partly resolved by such schemes as 'park and ride', leaving the car on the edge of town or 'kiss and ride', where the commuter's partner drives the car to and from the transport station.

Parking charges, which have long been a feature of urban motoring and originally served to 'ration' casual, on-street parking time are now a means of generating revenue and an important added cost to car users. It has been argued that, in spite of the apparent high level of current costs, the motorist is still, effectively, being subsidised. This approach has allowed the concept of 'road pricing', a toll to use city streets, to gain credence and development work is being carried out at a number of centres.

Because of the ingrained assumption of convenience and the high level of comfort and facilities offered by private cars, any realistic alternative will have to be of high quality in those

Street tramways operate through the elegant avenues of Bonn (Germany). In addition to street tramways the city also possesses a limited stop, high speed S-bahn system.

Like nearly all the Ruhr cities, Dusseldorf has retained and developed its tramway system alongside metro and bus services. Each mode fulfills a different purpose within the spectrum of an integrated public transport system.

terms. It will also need to be perceptibly less expensive for commuters to use than using their own vehicles on the urban section of their journey. To get to the edge of town they will still have to bear most of their existing costs.

In addition to the 'working commuters' there are the urban service users as well as residents. All these people need to move around within the town if not, necessarily, having to come into it from outside. Those who own cars often use them for short journeys for example taking children to school, shopping, visiting friends and for entertainment and leisure activities. If car use is to be restricted in urban areas (and it will eventually become self-restricting if no external agency acts first) the alternative will need to be extremely flexible.

Lisbon (Portugal) is in the process of introducing low floor articulated cars. Older, four-wheel cars have been retained to operate the steep and tortuous routes, some of which have the most severe gradients of any adhesion tramway on Earth. This particular example has been sold out of service to the Soller railway, Majorca.

It is doubtful whether any one mode of public transport can cater for all the requirements left if the private car were no longer so freely available. It is unnecessary to rely on only one alternative form of transport. Every system has its limitations and to ignore these is of no long term benefit to anyone.

It is the long-term benefit which needs to be considered. The costs involved in even the simplest of public transport schemes are high. It must be remembered that they can be laid-off over a varying number of years, depending on the mode. They will also generate some revenue. The potential benefits to the community and its individual members, as well as the enhanced quality of life, are equally valuable.

The style of Brussels' (Belgium) trams in service now show clear indications of descent from the early post-war cars which they have superseded. This car is preserved at Summerlee Museum, Scotland.

It is vital that an open approach is taken to the problem, seeking benefits to users, non-users and the environment over decades rather than months, or even years. A realistic and nonpartisan approach is the only one likely to achieve a solution.

Transport in Towns - Another Legacy.

Light Rail is a term which almost defies close definition, although the concept to which it applies is quite clear. Essentially, it refers to systems using steel rail and wheels, powered by electricity drawn from an overhead conductor and capable of operating either on street or reserved track. There are exceptions to each of these elements, though. Some light rail systems use third-rail conductors, some are diesel powered, others can only operate on reserved track or can share right of way with conventional railways.

The 'light' refers to the system's passenger capacity per hour compared with conventional, or 'heavy', railways as well as the weight of the vehicles used. The clearest way to define the concept is to consider the place of light rail in the spectrum of urban transport.

There are basically only two forms of transport depending on user accessibility; namely private and public. As well as the car, the private sector includes walking and cycling, both healthy activities requiring very little infrastructure beyond that already extant. As a daily commuting mode, though, they are distance-limited and not always convenient or practical if weather conditions are poor or if any kind of load needs to be carried. They are also inaccessible to a proportion of the population on physical grounds. The private car solves all these problems but, in turn, produces those of its own, outlined in "The Urban Environment". It is the excessive, uncontrolled use of this mode, to the detriment of others, which has led to many of the congestion

Reserved track between highway and pavement, Nantes (France).

Running round the trailers at Puerto Soller, Majorca. The line includes private reservation, street running and, as here, roadside operation. The line was constructed in order to extend the Palma to Soller railway to a distance where grants became available. Original rolling stock is still in use.

and environmental problems which now have to be solved in urban areas.

In the United Kingdom the two most commonly recognised forms of public transport are the bus and the train. These stand at opposite ends of the urban transport range as differentiated by each mode's hourly passenger capacity. There are no clear lines between the modes, each serving a different purpose in terms of capacity, service frequency and route distance. A well-considered urban transport policy would include appropriate examples from several categories, integrated to provide a total service.

Half-cab, rear entrance single and double-decker buses were common sights in most British cities up to a generation ago. These vehicles are preserved at the West of England Transport Collection, Winkleigh, Devon.

Traffic flow into and within urban areas is very much like a river with minor tributaries feeding larger ones until these combine into a number of clearly defined, permanent streams or corridors leading to the central business district. The inbound tidal flow of the morning is obviously reversed each evening. Throughout the day there is a relatively steady flow between centres within the urban area. The mode of public transport required must match likely flows and be upgradeable against future needs if it is to be successful.

Most modern buses are rear engined and have entrances at the front enabling one man operation. Southampton (UK).

Of the modes in the public transport spectrum the bus and its derivatives have the lightest passenger capacity per hour followed by light rail. Conventional railways (including 'Underground' and 'Metro' railways) have the greatest.

The bus comes in a variety of shapes, sizes and number of decks. Its capacity ranges from around 16 to just below 100 seats per vehicle. Almost without exception they are diesel powered, each requiring a driver who, in the UK at least, also usually collects fares. It has the advantage of route flexibility, serving where needed

as route requirements change. It competes for road space with all other road users and is therefore liable to delay. This has been ameliorated in part by the use of restricted ,'bus only' lanes, thereby reducing the road surface available to all other users by, in some cases, up to half. A service life of ten to fifteen years may be expected for a bus. The capacity per hour may be calculated from the number of seats passing a given stop in that time. 75 seater vehicles operating at two minute headway would provide a capacity of 2250 passengers per hour. At shorter headways it would become impossible to maintain timings and collect fares. The benefit of the bus is that it can be economical at much greater headways and, with smaller vehicles, on the outlying and feeder tributaries.

An early derivative was the electric trolley-bus, high capacity versions of which are still in service in many European towns. These require power stations and an infrastructure of overhead power cables, two wires in this case (one for earth) but are steered conventionally. Their capacity is about the same as for other buses but they lack route flexibility and cannot overtake the one in front. They are, however, pollution-free at point of use and quiet.

Guided buses are an attempt to gain the benefits of such transport whilst using reworked existing vehicle designs to retain route flexibility and save cost. For guidance, reserved 'track' is required which is then unavailable to other road users. On the guideway their capacity is about one-third greater than non-guided buses but, again, they cannot overtake without leaving the guideway, which renders the manoeuvre impossible. A development of this, the 'O bahn', requires massive and obtrusive guideways on totally reserved and virtually uncrossable 'track'.

In most parts of Europe single-deckers were favoured, often with more than one entrance/exit to reduce conflict of passenger flow at stops. These relatively recent Renault buses in Strasbourg follow this pattern.

Articulated buses enable higher passenger capacities from one man operation. Strasbourg (above) and Bilbao (Spain, below).

Guided Light Transit (GLT) is a recent approach to urban transport using rubber-tyred vehicles capable of being steered conventionally or guided by a grooved track set flush with the road surface. They are powered by electricity drawn by a pantograph from a double wire overhead whilst on the guideway and by a diesel engine elsewhere. Requiring dual control and power systems, they are heavy and complex vehicles, current versions being 100 seater, articulated, single-deckers. Their proclaimed advantage is that, at the end of the guideway, they possess the route flexibility of a conventional bus (except where limited by their size). At the extremities of routes, however, their capacity would be seriously under-used and their economics would suffer if they were not restricted to suitable core corridor routes. Additionally, they require reservations to gain a speed advantage or suffer the usual penalty of road-space competition. A realistic hourly capacity might be 4,000-5,000 passengers. Light rail covers a wide spectrum in terms of capacity and operation. Light rail vehicles (LRV) have steel, flanged wheels running on steel track. They may operate on the street, on reservations alongside it or on completely segregated track. Electrically powered, usually from an overhead conductor, they are suitable for operation on elevated viaducts, in tunnels and through pedestrian areas and enclosed malls. Capacity per hour ranges from 2,000-20,000 passengers. A thirty year service life is realistic. The adaptability of light rail makes it suitable for serving major corridors, its flexibility allowing systems to be inserted into the urban landscape with the minimum of structural alteration. On reserved or segregated track, light rail can improve journey times whilst various means of giving it priority can be used where it competes for road space, each LRV carrying the equivalent load to three buses or 200 cars.

Public transport and cycle lanes are becoming a feature of many cities in order to maintain timetables amidst increasing traffic congestion. Southampton.

Prior to deregulation of bus services this stop was served by Leicester Corporation. There is no common timetable or route pattern for the carriers who now call.

The ability to operate on-street reduces the necessity for segregated pathways in restricted city-centre space. It also makes it highly accessible whilst quietness of operation and lack of pollution at the point of use enhances the environment in which it operates. Light rail can offer real competition for the private car in terms of convenience, comfort and image. Where traffic flows are very heavy and where an urban area possesses a number of well-spread centres, usually in very large cities, the heavy rail metro comes into its own. Its nature requires such a system to occupy totally segregated, broad paths into urban areas or be placed under the ground.

Urban heavy rail vehicles operate in trains, usually electrically powered, serving stations much more widely spaced than those of other modes. Although a traffic capacity in excess of 50,000 passengers per hour is feasible, infrastructure costs are high, both financially and in land-take.

Heavy rail of a different type provides suburban access to city centres as well as links to long-distance interurban transport. Such systems appear ideal for bringing in large numbers of commuters from relatively great distances but suffer from under-usage between the morning and evening peaks.

Light rail fills the 'capacity gap' between bus and heavy rail 'metro'. Without it, corridors generating 2,000-20,000 passenger journeys per hour can only be served either inefficiently and inadequately or uneconomically. Light rail provides an answer to mass transportation problems in all but the largest urban areas and between specific centres in those.

Suburban trains still provide commuter services in many cities as here in Wuppertal, Germany, above, part of the integrated Ruhr system) and Bilbao, Spain (below).

Although the service between Soller and Palma (Majorca) operates as a conventional railway, the passenger carrying motor cars are, effectively, interurban trams. The approach to Palma station is made down the centre of the Eusebio Estada.

Light Rail and Guided Transport.

Having looked briefly at the systems available for the transportation of varying numbers of people it will be apparent that within the 'overlaps' between the modes there could be competition between them. Guided transport comes into its own where regular and frequent services are required over routes which are 'fixed' in the long term, rather than those which are being constantly amended or possess tremendously variable passenger levels.

Although guided transport is usually electrically powered, this is not exclusively the case. Vehicles powered by internal combustion engines are feasible (and used) as are 'dual system' vehicles. In some cases gravity and pumped water provide the power and, in others, electrically charged flywheels remove the need for an exposed power supply along the whole track. Some systems utilise a subsurface, endless cable (Llandudno in North Wales and San Francisco in the United States - although their systems are somewhat different). Neither is it necessary for guided transport to operate on conventional 'two-rail' track. Monorails have a long history; rubber-tyred systems, using either guide-beams or slots, are both in use.

Guided transport systems are also applicable to situations outside of urban areas, providing links to smaller, satellite centres, operating within theme parks and airports, providing transport along seafronts and piers. Some are not even essentially horizontal. Funicular railways, usually associated with 'cliff-lifts', also provide services in towns where there are drastic changes of level such as Lisbon (Portugal) and Bridgenorth (UK).

Surface rapid transit, operating as a conventional electric railway. Whilst Europe tended towards suburban railways and underground metros the United States also made extensive use of elevated, overhead systems. Cleveland, Ohio (USA).

Before the construction of 'heavy-rail' metros, Brussels built an extensive network of city centre tunnels for its trams. This 'pre-metro' is retained. Passengers board and alight on both sides of the car.

All these systems are responses to particular needs or problems and have occurred within the level of technology available at the time of their conception. This applies equally today. There are systems in current use which are over a century old; others whose technology is still virtually experimental. All are the result of endeavouring to provide for situations which arose at particular times. The period over which some of them have been operating indicates how correct the solution was.

Although the first-generation tramways in the United Kingdom had almost all closed by the 1960s, many of them had been operating for well over half a century, during which time enormous changes had occurred within the cities that they served. Within less than half that period the essential merits of the concept of guided, high-capacity transport has caused it to become seen as a solution to many of the problems which still exist in large urban areas, problems caused in part by the systems which were allowed to fill the gap left by the earlier closures.

The Marseilles Metro operates as 'heavy rail', fully signalled and segregated. Pneumatic tyres are used for the running gear.

Barcelona (Spain) has two separate metro systems, both using overhead current collection which is unusual on underground railways due to the necessarily increased tunnel diameter.

The Parry 'Peoplemover' uses kinetic energy stored in a flywheel to provide traction. This was an experimental demonstration in Brighton (Sussex) during 1994.

The Merry Hill (West Midlands) monorail linked stations within a shopping precinct to the car parks and a business centre on the same site.

The cable tramway at Shipley Glen has operated for more than a century carrying passengers to the moors above Bradford (Yorkshire).

Docklands Light Railway, over a century newer than Blackpool, is operated automatically linking the City with Stratford, Beckton and the Isle of Dogs.

Blackpool was the first town in the United Kingdom to introduce trams. The system is now restricted to a coastal route between Blackpool and Fleetwood but operates an intensive service. It has recently been re-equipped with new cars and overhead.

Double-deck car built around the components of an earlier vehicle. Blackpool 701 was designed to max-imise loadings from one-person operation. The body-work owes a great deal to contemporary bus prac-tice.

LIGHT RAIL AND GUIDED TRANSIT.

Section 2.

The Development of Guided Transport - A Bulletin History.

From the Middle Ages it was known that cart wheels ran more easily on wooden 'tracks' and this knowledge was applied to mining. Guidance could be provided by a raised edge to the boards and this, transferred to the wheel (as the flange), together with the application of steam power and iron rails, led to the beginnings of railway development.

The British Experience.

Street railways, horse-drawn and rail-guided, appeared in the early 1830s in the United States and in Paris during the 1850s. The vehicles resembled the railway carriages of the day and were not really suited to their role. During 1859 such a vehicle was operated briefly in Liverpool. The idea of a street passenger carriage of suitable design, with platforms at each of its identical ends, was again developed initially in the United States. Such vehicles did not need to be turned at each end of their route and could be entered and alighted from quickly and easily. They were introduced into Britain from the United States in 1860.

George Francis Train set up his first experimental tramway in Birkenhead in that year and followed these up with lines in London, Stoke and Arlington. The efficiency of metal wheels on rails was such that carrying additional passengers on the roof became possible. After a number of false starts - partly caused by Train's rails which projected above the road surface and were thus

Horse trams were introduced into Britain during the 1840s. A horse could draw far greater weight along rails than it could along the usual street surface of the day. The one control available was the chain operated handbrake (below).

dangerous to other road users and partly due to his business practices - the benefits of the concept became generally understood and further experiments with steam and continuous cable propulsion were made.

In 1883 Volk's Electric Railway opened in Brighton. Although not a street tramway, it demonstrated the possibilities of electric traction. Two years later, Blackpool became the first town in Britain to operate an electric street tramway, using a conduit pick-up method. Both these 'systems' still operate although Blackpool converted to a conventional overhead pick-up system in 1899. Electric tramways rapidly became popular, especially as the operators' power stations could also support street and domestic lighting as well. With low fares and reasonable speeds, the trams made the further expansion of towns possible.

In addition to tramways operated by city and town corporations, a number were built privately, often with leases for twenty-one years, after which there was an option to purchase by the local authority. British Electric Traction was amongst the leading exponents of this approach.

By 1927 there were over 14,000 tramcars operating in the United Kingdom. Although during the Edwardian period there had been a relatively limited number of vehicle and equipment producers, regrettably, many municipal operators later designed and built their own vehicles with little or no standardization (except in track gauge, and there were substantial differences even in that area). Trams tended to be well-built vehicles and their longevity, coupled with the rapid

Volk's Electric Railway, Brighton (UK) opened in 1883, the first electric transport system in Britain.

Early electric cars clearly demonstrated their horse-drawn ancestry. Indeed, some horse cars were later converted to electric operation.

advances in technology during the early years of the century, made them rapidly obsolete whilst still relatively new.

The growth in private car ownership was one factor in the gradual decline of the tram. Many vehicles became life-expired at the point when competition for road space in already cramped urban centres was becoming acute. Rather than meet the cost of renewal, system operators preferred to replace their trams with contemporary, flexible, new technology - the bus.

With the exceptions of Blackpool, the Great Orme and Shipley Glen (Bradford) cable tramways and Volk's Railway, which are still in operation, the last of the original systems to close were Sheffield in 1960 and Glasgow in 1962. It is interesting to note that the majority of today's urban corridor bus routes still follow the earlier tram routes.

Meanwhile, Across the Channel...

In parts of Europe the experience was very different. In Germany, where electric traction was effectively invented, operators had founded their still extant Association by the end of the Nineteenth century and, by the Thirties, had established a large measure of commonality and standardisation amongst systems and their components. This enabled longer production runs and greater opportunities for research and development. After the Second World War, when it became necessary to reconstruct the often severely damaged systems, the loaning of cars between undertakings was a practical proposition.

Four-wheeled, open-top cars - like this example preserved at Summerlee - introduced tram services in many UK towns and cities.

Trams and charabancs in The Square, Bournemouth (UK). As in many places modern bus routes continue to follow those of the trams.

Since 1991, this organisation has been known as the VDV (*Verband Deutscher Verkehrsbetriebse*) and continues to establish standards and designs for all aspects of tramway and light rail systems.

In the United Kingdom double-deck cars became common but, in Europe, single-deck cars towing one or more trailers fulfilled the accommodation requirements. In the days before off-vehicle ticket purchasing became common, a conductor was needed for each trailer. Although first tried in the United States, the articulated car was developed principally in Germany. Such cars, many with three or more sections, are now common on most new systems worldwide.

During the Nineteenth century, France was at the forefront of passenger transport experimentation. The first 'omnibuses' ran on the streets of Paris and by the 1870s attempts were being made to replace the horse as a means of propelling trams. Compressed-air was first tried in Nantes and later used in Paris and elsewhere. Some of these systems operated for nearly forty years.

Battery powered cars were also first tried in France in 1881. These proved unsuccessful due to the fumes which they produced and the weight of the cells as well as their limited range. In rural areas steam trams became common. Many of these were eventually replaced by diesel-powered vehicles where it was considered uneconomic to provide overhead electricity conductors.

Many of the centres which built new tramways displayed a high level of civic pride in their systems, exemplified in this traction pole base.

Barcelona, Spain.
The Tibidabo tramway is the vestigial remains of what was once an extensive system. The pre-Great War cars run on-street and collect power via trolley poles. Barcelona also possesses two independent underground metros and is planning a light rail system.

The decline amongst French tramways began later than in Britain but was effectively as complete. By the 1960s only three systems were still operating.

Both Belgium and Switzerland retained many of their systems. It is, perhaps, relevant that neither country has its own automobile industry. Switzerland was among the first European countries to develop standard trams for its various systems.

As well as urban systems, Belgium also possessed an extensive rural network. Whilst Brussels, Gent and other urban centres have retained their tramways, the rural lines have largely succumbed to road transport. Belgian companies also built and operated systems overseas, including El Qahira (Cairo). Many South American countries were supplied by Britain.

In eastern Europe until recently and in those countries with a centralised economy, the tram remained the mainstay of urban transport, with standardised vehicles built in their thousands, powered by cheap, coal-generated electricity. One of the most prolific producers was CKD-Tatra of Czechoslovakia (Praha is now in the Czech Republic) who built series of cars for both standard and metre-gauge systems throughout the then Warsaw Pact countries. Thousands are still in service although both Hungary and Russia produce their own cars.

Amongst others, systems also survived in Turin, Rome, Naples and Milan in Italy, Amsterdam, Rotterdam and The Hague in the Netherlands, Lille, Marseille and St. Etienne in France.

Preserved in Amsterdam (Netherlands), this four-wheeled car and trailer set is used for sightseeing tours.

The PCC car in its home environment. This is a relatively early car with 'standec' windows.

Many of these systems have been modernised and subsequently extended. In France new tramway or light rail systems have been constructed in Nantes, Grenoble, Paris, Rouen and Strasbourg. A number of automated systems, using rubber-tyred vehicles, have also been built, notably in Lille.

And on the Other Side of the Atlantic...

The concept of the horse-drawn tram was developed in the United States and many of the earliest cars in other parts of the world were built there, or locally under licence. The San Francisco cable-cars were the first of their kind when they were introduced in 1873. This system is still in operation and plans are in hand to reconstruct it as many of the cars have been in service for the equivalent of four or five expected working lives.

With the advent of electric traction, America remained in the forefront. The trolley-pole, by which current was collected from a single, overhead wire, was invented there during the 1880s by Charles van Depoele and improved during the same decade so that it rapidly became the world's standard system. American control equipment, motors and trucks were also widely used abroad during the early stages of tramway development.

In 1929, the presidents of twenty-five major American street-car undertakings held a conference from which stemmed the Presidents' Conference Committee (PCC). Its design team developed a standard car type, subsequently

East European practice is illustrated by Prague 180, preserved at the National Tramway Museum after being donated during the 1968 'Prague Spring'.

San Francisco cable cars at the junction of Powell and Hyde Streets soon after the Second World War. This system has remained largely intact since its inception despite the earthquake of 1906. A street funicular, the cars can be unclamped from the cable at the discretion of the driver.

known as the PCC car, whose safety and system standards formed the basis for most later American vehicles as well as for many built throughout Europe (including the ex-Warsaw Pact countries) up until the 1970s.

Subsequently, San Francisco, Boston and some others (including New Orleans which possesses the longest-lived tramway in the world, commencing operation in 1835) retained their systems whilst the majority fell to the familiar pattern of assault from the private car, lack of investment and the activities of what is now known as the 'road lobby'.

As in those areas of Europe where tramways were abandoned, there is now a desire to see the problems of urban traffic congestion and pollution solved. This has led to the construction of a number of new light rail and other electric-powered systems with more planned. Los Angeles, the city 'built on the automobile' has a new light rail system which is being extended into a network. Over half of the United States' systems have commenced operation in the last twenty years.

Canada also operates light rail or tramways in four cities - all but one being new in the last two decades of the Twentieth century. Mexico has three systems, all modern. There are few systems in South America but a number are planned.

The PCC car represented a major breakthrough in streetcar design. Sixty-odd years on cars of this type are still in use and many more modern vehicles owe much to PCC technology. Ghent (Belgium).

The drivers cab of a PCC-based car from Brussels. In addition to structural, motive power and braking improvements, a seat and instrumentation was provided for the driver, together with a public address system to inform passengers.

And Now...

Internationally, by the end of the 1970s, there were just under three hundred systems worldwide, of which more than half were in the then 'Eastern Bloc' countries or Germany.

Since 1978, nearly fifty completely new systems have opened whilst nearly twice as many are under construction, authorised or planned. These figures do not include other guided transport systems such as bus guideways, monorails or people-movers.

By way of comparison, eighty-six cities possess heavy rail urban transit systems of which thirty-two are new. Some cities, notably Amsterdam and Zurich, have ceased heavy rail 'metro' construction by popular demand, and concentrated on light rail development.

Zurich has had trams for over a century. The Tram 2000 design is intended to operate on the existing system, replacing older cars.

Trams are being reintroduced in many cities in Europe and the United States. Stasbourg's system is completely new.

*Enhancing the environment. Grenoble 2024 passing
the Lycee Stendahl.*

LIGHT RAIL AND GUIDED TRANSIT.

Section 3. The Technology.

Most modern existing and proposed systems are usually feted as being 'high tech.' as, probably, were the first electric tramcars in their day.

The idea of guidance by rail has been understood for possibly two millennia; the wheel for far longer and electricity as an applied power source for nearly two centuries. The original conjunction of these ideas into the concept of the tram occurred well over one hundred years ago. The basis of modern tramways, light rail and guided transit systems is well-tried, clearly understood and reliable technology.

Development and improvement must inevitably involve a measure of new and experimental approaches. Long before any of these are used in passenger service they have been tested, approved and shown to work safely.

The word used to describe the whole physical set-up of a tramway, light rail or guided transit network is 'system'. Vehicles cannot operate without their guide tracks, power supplies and control mechanisms. They cannot transport passengers without stops, ticket machines, signing and marketing organisations. All the parts of a modern system are usually integrated from the outset. They are also usually conceived with extension and eventual improvement in mind.

The first-generation tramways tended to have very long service lives. There is no reason to suspect that current systems will have shorter ones.

Gare Europole, Grenoble (France). The tramway, soon to be extended, uses the latest technology and provides a standard often used to judge later systems.

Place Commerce, Nantes (France). Nantes was the first French city to reintroduce trams.

Cars and Other Rolling-Stock.

To the system user and, in the case of tramways, road users as well, the cars are the most immediately apparent element.

In the UK, prior to the closure of the first-generation systems, these tended to be single vehicles, usually double-ended, double-deckers mounted on either a single, four-wheel truck or two, four-wheel bogies. Single deckers were also common where traffic levels were lower or where such hazards as railway over-bridges demanded low height.

Power was usually collected from the overhead contact wire by a trolley pole. Exits and stairs were normally at each end and, on many vehicles, the driver was required to stand. There was a similarity of style which stemmed from the earlier horse-drawn trams.

In Europe single-deck vehicles were the norm. Early examples were mounted on four-wheel trucks and towed a trailer when additional capacity was necessary. Similar vehicles were used in the United States. Eight-wheel vehicles (mounted on two bogies) eventually became common but retained the single deck.

To overcome the necessity of carrying more than one conductor, experiments were carried out linking two four-wheelers together with a suspended centre section. This early form of articulation was referred to as 'two rooms and a bath'. In Germany this led the way to six-axle (three bogie), articulated vehicles with the inner ends of the two sections supported on a common truck. If necessary, a trailer could be attached to these cars.

Tramways possess historical continuity in Switzerland where they have developed steadily. This postwar standard car operates in Basle.

Zurich (Switzerland) is considered by some to be the tramway capital of the world! Its extensive (and intensive) services are operated by modern articulated cars but museum vehicles are used on special excursions.

The longevity of vehicles, their continuing ability to fulfil their original purpose and the cost and rapidity of change in new cars led to older rolling stock being retained. As systems replaced vehicles which were often far from time-expired, so these were sold on to other systems. Several undertakings in eastern Europe have benefited from this and now operate second-hand, but still relatively modern, cars passed on by western operators.

In several areas, particularly where systems have had a continuous history, bogie cars and two-section articulated cars (with and without trailers) are still in use, as are some earlier, four-wheeled cars. Plans often exist to replace these with new vehicles. Many undertakings retain examples of earlier stock as museum cars, not necessarily to be displayed as a static exhibit.

Private hire, wedding and party cars, sightseeing and even restaurant cars are operated in a variety of places in Germany, Switzerland and further east. Articulated cars form the basis of most modern light rail and tramway vehicles. Three section (eight axle) vehicles are developed from them (often by adding a centre section to an existing vehicle) and recent deliveries of four and five section vehicles have been made.

Works' fleets often include recovery vehicles (sometimes with auxiliary diesel power), tower wagons for maintaining overhead equipment

Basle has an extensive tramway system and has used articulated cars for over thirty years. To increase capacity many draw trailers.

Manchester was the first city in the UK to reintroduce street-running trams, high-floor, articulated cars requiring platforms in the street for level entry.

Double-articulated (three section) car in Freiburg (Germany). A development of a standard post-war design, these cars are now being replaced by low-floor vehicles.

and rail grinders to remove corrugations which develop in the track. In systems built from new, these vehicles will be purpose designed. In older systems they are often based on earlier passenger service cars.

Construction.

Early vehicles were constructed of timber. A frame of ribs and stringers (often of teak) was covered with panels (usually mahogany). Other timbers were sometimes used including ash and oak. The body shape was retained in part by the bulkheads but principally by the quality of the joinery work. The body was mounted on a steel truck (or longitudinal girders with a swivelling truck, or bogie, at each end). By the 1930s it was common to build the framework of steel with panelling of either the same material or aluminium.

There is a variety of materials in use in current production cars. Steel is most commonly used for body frames and panels although some vehicles are constructed throughout from aluminium. The majority of these tend to be for use on track which is reserved from other traffic. Aluminium cars are often built on the monocoque principle with no separate chassis and the running gear carried on sub-frames. Most cars in steel have separate under-frames which not only provide attachment for the trucks but often also carry much of the ancillary equipment. Cars produced in the UK for operation in Strasbourg are amongst the first to use glass-reinforced plastic panels fixed to the steel frame by loop and hook fasteners. These cars are also the first production vehicles to be designed and built on a modular basis.

In addition to passenger vehicles, systems require works cars. This one, at Seaton (Devon), is used for line and overhead maintenance and towing.

Three-section car in Berne, Switzerland demonstrating how sharply curved the track can be. Each articulation has a truck beneath it.

The sections of the car are joined by a permanent, flexible coupling which is usually mounted on the centre truck. There is a wide variety of different approaches to this. In some cars built for new tramways in France, there is a short centre section between the main sections of the car. The centre truck is mounted beneath this. There are, thus, two flexible connections and the car has, in effect, three sections.

Trams in Geneva and elsewhere have a centre truck, with small wheels, mounted beneath the inner end of one section rather than the articulation itself. CKD-Tatra articulated cars have a single truck mounted centrally beneath each body section and are thus eight-wheelers. The trucks are coupled independently as well as by the articulated body. The ABB cars for Strasbourg have their wheels beneath the cab sections at the ends and the articulation modules elsewhere. The main body sections are suspended between these.

Access.

Early cars were normally built double-ended, that is both ends were identical and the vehicle could be driven from either. Such cars are suitable where there are no turning circles at the route ends. Where there are turning circles, single-ended cars may be used. As well as saving the space otherwise occupied by the second cab and requiring less control equipment, such cars only need near-side doors.

In Britain, traditional cars had platforms at each end by which passengers boarded. The driver's controls were also placed here as were the stairs to the upper deck. Originally, these platforms were protected only by a curved dash

From the passengers point of view the articulation between sections is fully enclosed. This car, in Geneva (Switzerland), has two trucks under one section and one under the other, thus providing a floating articulation.

Grenoble cars have a truck-supported centre section articulated at both ends between the main sections.

panel but later cars were provided with canopies and windscreens (not universally liked by drivers as safety glass was not available at that time). The entrance remained open on most cars in spite of these improvements. Passengers were prevented from using the platform, at whichever was the front, by a sliding door in the saloon bulkhead.

In Europe, trams were fitted with doors from a much earlier date, though some retained open entrances. All modern vehicles are fitted with doors operated either electrically or pneumatically.

A number of different door types are in use. Many older vehicles have double-doors which fold back against the vestibule sides. Others are fitted with 'butterfly' doors, two single panels which swing back in an arc to fit against the sides of the vestibule when open. These, like folding doors, can be very inconvenient for passengers standing nearby, although this part of the entrance is often occupied by the steps needed to mount the car from kerb level.

The usual practice is to fit doors which are either of the 'plug' type, which swing out and back parallel to the vehicle sides, or sliding doors mounted on tracks on the outer skin. It is impractical to fit outward-opening doors because of the danger they represent to intending passengers at stops.

It is usual for all doors (or pairs of doors) to be operated by users. Clearly marked push-buttons or pads are supplied on both the inside and the outside of the vehicle. This way, only the doors in use for that particular stop are opened

Strasbourg's (France) new system has state-of-the-art cars with electronic control, low floors and extensive use of loop fasteners for the glass fibre panelling.

which saves on heating or air conditioning within the car. Indicators in the cab let the driver know which are open. Some vehicles cannot be moved unless all the doors are closed. Drivers are provided with mirrors (sometimes retractable when the car is moving) so that they can carry out a visual check before moving off. All doors are at least part-glazed, often down to a level with the interior floor.

The Low-Floor Trend.

A fundamental difference, from the passengers' point of view, between street-running trams and heavy railways, is the height difference between the kerb and the vehicle floor. In the past this has been overcome by steps (almost vertical in the early days.) These have obvious disadvantages not only for mobility impaired passengers but also for those encumbered with luggage, shopping or with small children and pushchairs.

A range of ideas has been tried to overcome this. The most obvious is the construction of level-height platforms with approach ramps at boarding places. Apart from the additional cost involved, such structures are not practical where the vehicles are operated in the street. They are acceptable where reserved track is the norm but cannot solve the problem if the system has any on-street stops.

To partially overcome the difficulty 'profiled' platforms have been tried. These have two levels, a short, upper level serving one or two doors and a longer, kerb-height section for the remainder. The street-running sections of the Manchester system are provided with these. They require the stops to be at the kerbside rather than in the

Double unit of different era cars in Basle (Switzerland). The steps lower automatically as the twin-leaf doors fold back.

'Butterfly' doors on this Centenary class car in Blackpool fold back into the step well.

Exterior sliding doors fitted to a Docklands train.

roadway and the higher section occupies a considerable amount of pavement space, restricting pedestrian passage to a certain extent. They also tend to segregate those who require this ease of access from other passengers.

Some systems (including San Diego, California) have tried driver-operated lifts at stops. Apart from the segregation effect, these require time to operate, thus slowing the system down. Retractable, sloping ramps to the door nearest the cab are a feature on many systems, including Grenoble, France. These ramps are relatively short and can be automatic, extending as the door opens, but are usually driver-operated for safety reasons.

The ideal answer is to provide a vehicle whose floor is at the same height as the boarding point pavement. In practice this has proved more difficult to achieve than might be apparent. Much of the equipment traditionally mounted under the floor can be carried on the roof of the car. Access then requires an overhead gantry at the depot. Alternatively much of it can be concealed in cabinets within the saloons.

Regardless of how much is repositioned in this manner, the wheels must remain underneath. As these are normally grouped in pairs on a common, solid axle, in turn paired on a truck, at least some of the floor (in the centre aisle) has to clear the height of the top of the axle. The upper parts of the wheels, truck and so on, may be concealed under seat podia or longitudinal seating. Alternatively, the floor at the ends of the car can be raised to allow for the running gear. These areas, away from the doors may be used by passengers travelling longer distances whilst the areas near the doors can be dropped to near kerb height.

Wide sliding doors on Strasbourg's cars enable rapid entry and exit whilst individual control reduces heating loss from the car during winter.

Even with retractable steps access for the mobility-restricted can be quite difficult in older vehicles. Basle, Switzerland.

Where articulated cars have a central truck the low-floor area will necessarily be split. In order to attain an overall low floor the trucks, motor and transmission systems needed to be completely reconsidered.

Running Gear.

The running-gear on early trams derived mainly from traditional railway practice. A pair of steel wheels was fixed one to each end of a solid axle such that the unit rotated as a whole. The ends of the axles, where they protruded through the centres of the wheels, were mounted in axle boxes containing a bearing. Often these were white metal journals which required constant greasing.

Two such axles were mounted on a common truck at a distance apart suitable to the curves encountered on the route. The tighter the curves, the shorter the wheelbase. All the brake gear, motors and other necessary equipment was also attached to the truck. This meant that the floor of the lower saloon was quite high off the ground and required two or three steps to enter.

The use of one truck restricted the length, and hence the passenger capacity of the car, there being a limit to how much could overhang at each end. One answer was to provide so called 'radial' trucks. These had two axles which could turn at an angle to each other when going around curves. In practice these suffered from rapid wear. The solution was to provide two short trucks (or bogies) pivoted beneath the saloon floor. This allowed longer vehicles to be built without much detracting from their ability to take sharp curves.

To overcome the 'high-floor' difficulty Manchester uses profiled platforms at street stops enabling level access to the forward section of the car.

Berne has introduced low-floor cars with entry at kerb level. They utilise trucks with small wheels to reduce floor height.

It did nothing to lower the floor. This approach has been retained up to the present time for the majority of cars.

In an effort to gain the most benefit from the available motors without having to provide one per axle, a design of bogie was developed with driving wheels (on the motored axle) larger than the pony wheels. The mounting pivot was placed towards the driving axle to provide better adhesion. This type was known as a 'maximum traction' bogie.

Practice in the United States tended towards equal wheel bogies with each axle powered. This approach was adopted in the UK particularly (but not exclusively) for systems with hilly routes where the additional power was of benefit. Amongst suppliers of trucks, the American company of J.G. Brill is possibly one of the best known. Equipment supplied by them, or their licensees, was used all over the world and much of it is still in service. Essentially similar trucks continue to be the usual running-gear on a majority of cars today.

Modular cars of the Mannheim (above) and Ludwigshafen (below) systems.

The wheels themselves, originally cast-iron, were later commonly fitted with a steel tyre. This provided greater resistance to wear and proved cheaper in the long run than replacing the entire wheel. More recently cast wheels were replaced by pressed steel. During the 1930s, the PCC car included in its specification the use of resilient inserts in the wheels between the hub and tyre. Resilient wheels provide a far quieter ride together with measures of absorption for vibration and suspension. Such wheels are now virtually universal.

During the last quarter of the Twentieth century there have been revolutionary changes in the way that wheels, suspension and motors have been considered.

The convention of pairs of wheel-sets with motors driving rotating axles, all grouped in a pivoted truck, has begun to give way to concepts involving independently rotating wheels with motors mounted on the body of the car or, in other cases, outside the wheel hub or within the wheel itself. Such solutions enable each wheel to be driven or, where this is unnecessary, for cars with genuinely low floors to be developed.

As in many industries there was an element of traditionalism amongst tram and light rail vehicle builders and operators. The essential difficulty to be overcome in producing a low floor over the entire saloon was that, whatever other equipment went in cabinets or on the roof, the wheels and motors had to remain underneath. The continued use of trucks meant that, even if the wheel tops could be covered with seat podia, the floor (or at least part of it across the whole width of the car) had to be high enough to clear the axles and motors.

It is by rethinking the basis of the running-gear that low-floor vehicles have become a practical proposition. Efforts during the 1970s and 80s concentrated on providing as much low floor area as possible in the spaces between the trucks and on fitting new centre sections (and an additional bogie) to existing two-section, articulated cars.

Ludwigshafen (Germany) is one of several operators which has added low-floor centre sections to some existing cars thus improving access and extending their service lives.

Conventional four-wheeled tram truck (one of a pair) beneath car 14 on the Seaton and District Tramway.

PCC cars were mounted on trucks with resilient wheels and powerful, electromagnetic track brakes.

This could allow up to about a third of the floor to be at approximately the height of the loading kerb but both solutions segregate those with a requirement for stepless access, so as to reach the car ends, or to pass from one section to another, steps had to be mounted. In addition, by the nature of the design, encumbered passengers are required to stand, effectively, in the door vestibules - the area most desirable to be kept clear for rapid boarding and alighting.

An alternative, which allowed for access between the sections, is to provide a 'small-wheel' bogie beneath the articulation. In practice such trucks usually support the ends of a section, with the articulation 'floating'. The floor height still depends on the axle height but up to two-thirds of the area can be at, or near, boarding height.

The current trend is to provide an overall low floor by designing the running gear in such a way that it does not intrude into the saloons except where it can be covered by fixtures such as seat podia.

To achieve this a number of innovative ideas have been tried, more or less successfully. In each case, means have been found to reduce the height requirement across the car interior between the wheels.

The Belgian car manufacturers BN have developed a 'radial' bogie with the motors integrated with the wheels, effectively outside the bogie. In this design the wheels not only rotate separately but also pivot in pairs reducing the rotational requirement of the bogie relative to the car for any given curve. The wheels have no central, mid-height axle between them. The parts of the truck which join the two sides are kept low.

PCC cars remain in use in Brussels (above) and Marseilles amongst other cities.

Marseilles PCC-based single unit cars are fitted with few seats in order to carry large numbers of standees. Access is by folding doors and steps at each end of the saloon. The floor is flat and level.

A German solution, developed by VDV and known as the EEF *(Einze/rad Einzel Fahrwerk)* wheelset has single, independent wheels, again with integrated motors where they are driven. Each wheel is self-steering, controlled by the interaction of the wheel profile and the track. The non-powered, or trailing, design has been shown to work effectively but the powered version has been less successful and no cars using it have yet been ordered for public service. Development continues.

Further solutions with body-mounted motors driving pairs of wheels through cardan-shafts and gearboxes are proving successful, enabling a level, low gangway throughout the vehicle.

Low-floor cars with various degrees of innovation represent a majority of recent acquisitions and orders.

Track.

Next to the vehicles themselves, the track upon which they run is the most noticeable feature to an observer. (If it is the overhead then it may be considered too intrusive.) Where the track is segregated from other users, such as on private rights of way, railway practice can be applied with sleeper-based rails and ballast. In other situations different approaches are necessary.

Street-based track is of the grooved type. Usually the profile is formed in the top of a steel girder between 15 and 20cm. deep. The base of the girder is beneath the surface with only the grooved top showing. The rails are kept at the right gauge by steel cross-members. The laying of this kind of track requires the movement

Sheffield's trams have low-floor sections between the doors and high-floor sections, reached by steps, at the car ends.

St. Etienne (France) has introduced low-floor cars with floating articulations. Unusually, they are equipped with trolley poles.

of all underground services such as water mains and power cables from beneath the area to be occupied. Repair or replacement of such track is a major undertaking.

On many new systems the rails are laid in grooves cut in the top surface of a concrete raft. The rails are much shallower as they do not require the strengthening web of the girder track. They are held in place by clips, resilient inserts between the rail and the side of the groove or by a mastic compound which also helps to insulate them and reduce sound caused by vibration. A number of different track systems are being tried in an effort to reduce initial and maintenance costs, extend rail life and cut down on noise.

Track is usually formed on-site but pointwork and complex curves (including those with a change of angle vertically as well as horizontally) are usually built at the factory and reassembled where required. Track panels, in which the complete track unit, including the base, is prefabricated and placed in a shallow trough excavated on site, is another approach. This system is designed to reduce disruption, save site costs and to ease maintenance and replacement. The completed track will have a bonded steel mesh beneath it to cope with any electrical leakage.

Although grooved track is normally used for street-running, some applications use ordinary, flat-bottomed rail laid in troughs and sealed with mastic in which the groove is formed alongside the rail head. Alternatively a second rail may be laid alongside to act as a check rail, which is the primary purpose of the groove in conventional tram rail.

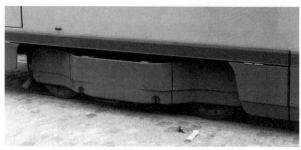

Early tramcars had their wheels protected by such devices as drop trays and dog bars. In most modern vehicles the truck design is such that hardly any of the wheel is exposed at all. Rouen (France).

Complex trackwork at the entrance to Sheffield's Nunnery Depot was fabricated off-site and reassembled in position.

Where track is in areas shared with other traffic (including pedestrian precincts) it normally has the area 'swept' by the cars differentiated in some way. This may be with coloured pavior, granite setts, a differently textured surface or even grass.

The rail profile (the shape of the surface upon which the wheel runs) is different from railway track. The angle of the tyre is often flatter and the rail's running surface matches this. Tram and light rail vehicle wheels have shallower flanges than railway vehicles. On points and crossings the vehicle often runs on the wheel flange so the bottom surface of the groove is built-up at these places.

Trams have always had to fit into existing urban environments, with tight curves around corners and relatively steep gradients. Light rail continues this tradition in that it can be fitted into existing surroundings with a minimum of disruption, demolition and construction of major civil engineering projects to support it.

Power Supply.

The basic circuitry by which trams, light rail and other forms of electric vehicle operate is essentially simple. Power, taken from the source via an overhead cable (or third rail), is collected by the vehicle through a pick-up (usually either a trolley-head, pantograph or collection shoe), fed through the motors and earthed through the track (or a second cable in the case of vehicles running on pneumatic tyres) from where it returns to the source.

Between the pick-up and motors there are two switches - the main power breaker which acts as a safety switch, in case of overload, and the

Grass-sown track where the line runs on roadside reservation in Basle.

Paved track on the Docklands Light Railway.

Temporary track laid on the street surface for a Parry 'Peoplemover' Demonstration.

controller which controls the power to the motors and hence the speed of the vehicle. In practice the system is much more complex than this, a wide range of subsystems often being employed to operate signalling, priority lights, points, status information for the control centre, lighting and passenger information both on and off the car. The basics, though, still comprise a power source, a pick-up, control switches, motors and earthed rails (or cables.)

Early tramways were supplied with power from generating stations, usually owned by the undertaking's operator. Where this was a local authority, they very often supplied street lighting as they owned both the power station and the lineside traction poles. Many undertakings still produce their own electricity supplies. Others take a supply from the national grid, which has to be stepped-down to the required voltage.

A majority of systems use direct current (DC) at between 600 and 750 volts (this being the European standard) although there are exceptions. On some systems which are completely segregated, alternating current (AC) is used. There are examples of systems which use both, AC for segregated parts of the line, DC where it runs in the street. Vehicles on these systems are 'switchable' between the types of current but are necessarily more complex. AC requires fewer sub-stations but DC is more easily controlled.

Overhead and Other Methods of Collection.

The usual method of distributing power to the vehicles is through an overhead cable. This consists of a single (or occasionally double) copper cable suspended above the track.

In Grenoble large sections of street track are surrounded by coloured surfacing to show the area swept by the cars as they pass.

Nantes uses more conventional stone setts with a distinctive colour and texture to indicate the swept area.

Rosette attachment in Soller (Majorca).

At intervals the wire is held by clips (known as 'ears') to insulated brackets attached to traction poles. The poles may also support street lights, signal lights and road signs. Where possible, the overhead conductor wire is held by wires (spanwires) across the track. These are attached through insulators to brackets (rosettes) fixed to buildings. This reduces the need for street or pavement space alongside the route and allows a less cluttered environment.

Conventional overhead on the Seaton tramway. Frequent 'pull-offs' are required to negotiate curves in order to retain the conductor wire within the swing limits of the trolley pole.

Whilst the track may curve, the overhead has to follow by a series of straight sections with angles between them. This can be accomplished by reducing the distance between the traction poles or rosettes and providing pull-offs to change the conductor's direction and maintain its tension. The conductor must follow the centre of each track as closely as possible and not extend beyond the 'swept' area if pantographs are used as pick-ups, as these cannot swing out like trolley-poles.

The power is collected via a pick-up mounted, in the case of overhead collection, on top of the car. A trolley head (which may be a carbon block or a brass pulley wheel) mounted at the end of a pole pivoted where it is mounted on the car roof, is the traditional method. The trolley pole allows current to be collected from a wire which is not directly above the track.

A less complex form of this is the bow-collector. Unlike the trolley pole, it does not require turning at the end of the route. The wire can simply be mounted slightly higher so that the bow comes upright at the end of the line. As the vehicle moves off in the opposite direction, so the bow takes up the correct angle. The conductor must be over the track for bows to work.

Traction poles in Manchester. Where possible the spanwires are attached to buildings to reduce visual intrusion by the poles.

The most popular method for modern vehicles is to fit a pantograph. Like bow-collectors, they are fitted with carbon skids which are held at right-angles to the vehicle's direction of travel by a flexible, sprung frame. This may be raised or lowered from inside the car but, when extended in service, it can rise and fall to allow for changes in height of the overhead conductor. Pantographs usually require the overhead to be heavier duty and held in greater tension than the other types of collector. They cannot usually, though, come off the wire.

Pantographs are the usual current collectors on modern cars. This is an older design in use in Blackpool.

Where an overhead system was thought to be unsightly, conduit collection was used. The very first electric street tramway (Blackpool) started using this method. The conductor was contained in an open-topped tube between the rails. A slot, either adjacent to one rail or in the centre, allowed a 'plough', connected to the car, to pick up current. Blackpool changed to the overhead system because the trough became easily clogged with sand. Places like Bournemouth and London retained it for longer. Also tried in the early days were self-activating studs. These were abandoned because they did not always deactivate and remained live after the car had passed by.

Where systems are completely segregated from other road users and passengers have no access to the running track, a 'third rail' conductor can be used. This is mounted adjacent to the running rail and the current is collected by a 'shoe' which slides along the surface. The 'shoe' normally runs on top of the rail but Docklands Light Railway, for example, has the third rail suspended on low brackets and shrouded with the shoe being pressed to the lower surface.

Single-arm pantograph on a Sheffield car.

Provided that there are a sufficient number of pick-up shoes on the car, it is possible to allow gaps in the conductor for access and crossings or to alternate sides. The conductor's continuity is maintained by cables linking the ends of visible sections through underground conduits.

Having been generated, conducted, collected and applied to moving the vehicle, the current is earthed through the running rails. These are connected to the source thus completing the circuit. For vehicles using pneumatic tyres or concrete track or guideways, a different earthing system is employed. Either there is a second trolley pole and cable (as in trolley-buses) or the track contains a steel, copper or aluminium strip with an earthing shoe on the vehicle.

The third-rail conductor on the Docklands Light Railway is protected by a shroud with the shoe collecting current from the underside.

Motors.

The motors which power electric railways of all kinds are exactly the same, in principle, as the domestic ones running washing machines, blenders and hair dryers.

In early trams the motors were usually of the four-pole type, completely enclosed and non-ventilated. This meant that they generated a good deal of heat and could not be run at their maximum efficiency. Improvements took place throughout the early part of the century including the addition of 'commutator poles' which reduced spark damage within the motor. The application of forced air ventilation, initially by the simple expedient of adding a fan to the motor shaft, allowed great increases in both constant and short term power ratings from the same size of motor. New materials for insulation and

Shielded conductor sections at stops provide power for a motor to 'spin-up' the flywheel in the Parry system.

cases enabled smaller, lighter and more powerful motors to be developed.

The three-phase, DC motors in use today are usually 'nose hung' to the truck at right-angles to the axle and drive through right-angle gearboxes. In some designs they are mounted outside the truck, within the wheel-hub or hung within the car body and drive through a shaft. Each motor usually drives one axle but there are designs in which both axles are geared to a single motor and others in which each wheel is driven independently.

Control Systems.

As it is impractical to connect motors directly to the circuit, some kind of mechanism is necessary to prevent damage from electrical surges, to control the current and hence the speed.

The earliest practical method (and one still in use today on some older cars and many operating in museums) was to provide resistance in the circuit which could be progressively removed in steps as the vehicle gathered speed.

This was accomplished by a removable handle mounted at the top end of a shaft which physically altered the resistance as it was moved from notch to notch. The same controller handle could normally be moved beyond the top of the 'series' notches to link the motors in 'parallel'. In series the power passes from one motor to the next before earthing, in parallel both motors are fed simultaneously.

Directional control was provided by a 'key', again removable, on an adjacent shaft. The whole mechanism was enclosed within a steel pillar which provided protection from sparks.

The controls on older trams comprised a directional switch (forwards or backwards) operated by a removable key, a controller handle which removed resistances from the circuit as the car accelerated and a manual handbrake.

The cab of a Sheffield car. Direction, speed and braking are all controlled by one handle.

As more powerful motors became available this method became less suitable. In addition it suffered from jerkiness as each notch was encountered. These steps could lead to a less than comfortable ride.

To enable more powerful motors to be used satisfactorily, cam operated contractors were developed. These could be operated by air. The control handle itself could be reduced in size and the equipment it operated could be placed elsewhere than on the platform.

The system used on PCC cars in the 1930s employed a multi-notch rheostat with up to ninety-nine positions, motor operated. This enabled the driver to effectively preset the rate of acceleration without the noticeable 'steps'.

Solid-state electronics have allowed much more effective control to be applied and have reduced power wastage. 'Chopper' control, using gate-turn-off thyristors, which very rapidly cuts-off and restores power, allows the use of a single lever for acceleration, cruising and braking. The lever may be set anywhere within its range and the car will simply accelerate to that speed. The dangers of overloading and blowing out the main trip have largely disappeared. Acceleration is now stepless.

Safety Systems - Brakes.

Once the car is moving, it is obviously imperative that it can be brought to a controlled halt. This must be achieved, in normal service, in a manner which does not create problems for standing passengers or those already moving towards the doors.

The motors powering cars on the Wuppertal Schwebebahn are apparent for all to see. Trams and light rail vehicles have similar motors usually mounted within the truck. In some low floor cars the motors are mounted on the body frames and transmit to the wheels via flexible shafts.

Electromagnetic track brakes provide a very powerful means of stopping the car in an emergency.

To save space beneath the floor the disc brakes on this Berne car are mounted outside the wheels.

There are, basically, four types of brakes. Early cars had a simple, manual brake operated by a rotating handle in a frame on the platform. Turning this worked a system of chains and levers which drew steel brake-blocks into contact with the wheels' tyres. The levers ensured that it was possible for reasonable pressure on the brake handle to be 'stepped-up' sufficiently to halt several tonnes of tram. Such brakes could also be used for parking. A handle was fitted at each end and, when the car was operated in the opposite direction, the driver had to first apply the brake at the other end before releasing what had now become the rear brake, which had been applied on arriving.

Trams do not have priority at this level crossing between Blackpool and Fleetwood.

Electric, or rheostatic braking was also available on early cars and continues to be used. By turning the controller handle back beyond the stop notch, the system was wired to cause the motors to act as generators. This created a powerful braking force on the wheels and also fed power thus generated back into the conductor cable. Where a number of vehicles were operating on a section, this additional power could be usefully applied to their acceleration.

Track brakes act on the rail top, not on the wheels. They are applied either by springs or magnetically and work by simple friction. Where they are operated in concert with any brakes acting on the wheels it is necessary to provide an interlock system as they reduce wheel adhesion when they are applied.

In spite of theoretical tramway priority the sharing of road space in Brussels sometimes leads to unwise manouevres.

Shoe or disc brakes operated by air are now more or less standard. They have the advantage of being both extremely powerful and controllable. Air pressure is supplied by an electric pump.

A difficulty experienced on all steel-wheel, steel-railed vehicles is that of slippage on wet track. To overcome this when braking, accelerating or encountering steep gradients, sanders are fitted. These spray a small amount of dry, fine sand onto the track in front of the wheels. This increases the grip available. Modern cars are fitted with automatic, electronic slip and skid control and anti-lock brakes.

Other Safety Aspects.

On early cars safety was entirely in the hands of the crew and depended on both their awareness and state of health. Vehicles operating on modern systems still rely on this but include a number of additional features.

It is quite possible (though scarcely legal) to set up an older tram at a given speed, take the driver's hands from the controls and allow it to drive itself. Should any misfortune affect the driver, the car will continue until stopped by the end of the track unless the conductor, if there is one, takes over. The fitting of a 'dead man's' handle, or pedal, prevents this danger. This consists of a switch which must be kept open manually for the car to operate. If it is released it springs off, closes down the power and applies the brakes.

Earlier systems relied on 'line-of-sight' operation. That is, cars were driven within margins of safety dictated by the conditions which the driver could see. These days this is no longer sufficient. On segregated lines, signalling and single track tokens have been used from the first.

Where vehicles share road space with other traffic, even where this consists of simply crossing roads before entering reserved track, some form

In Sheffield trams do receive priority at road crossings.

Although Docklands Light Railway cars are automatic the track still carries visual restriction signs for use when cars are being manually driven. The mirror is for the Train Captain to check the doors.

of signalling is essential. Rail vehicles cannot go where there is no track, they are therefore hampered when compared with other road vehicles. The signalling which is used needs to be distinct from that applying to other road traffic. Visual signals usually consist of two rows of at least three white lights arranged in a cross. This is shrouded against reflection and glare from sunshine. When the horizontal row is lit it forms a bar which indicates that the vehicle may not proceed. Lighting the vertical row indicates that the vehicle may proceed. At junctions it is possible to indicate the track which the car will follow. These signals may be connected to signals for other traffic in a way which gives the tram priority.

Each country which possesses trams or light rail systems has developed forms of standard signs as warnings or indicators of the system's presence or priority. This often consists of a stylised side elevation of a tram. Sometimes a front view is used. In all cases it is important that it is immediately distinguishable. Some country's signs are more elegant than others.

Where Highway Codes, or their equivalent, are available a section on trams will be included providing information relevant to other road users. As well as priorities and reserved track this may include the information that the tram cannot swerve out of the way.

The essential safety feature of light rail and guided transit vehicles lies in their inherent strength of design and construction, being, typically, steel framed and relatively large.

Basle (Switzerland) city and suburban tramway cars. The junction adjacent to this stop has a tram passing about every ten seconds at peak times.

Blackpool Tower enjoys an intensive service at the height of summer.

The interior of the car, open plan in design, is within view of the driver who is, in turn, in radio contact with the system's control room giving greater personal security.

Stops, which usually include covered shelters, timetable information and, increasingly, constantly updated service status information, can be fitted with closed-circuit television so that they, too, can be monitored from the control room.

Light rail, tramway and guided vehicles have smoother ride qualities than most road vehicles enabling standing passengers to travel more comfortably and in greater safety.

Design Purpose and Parameters.

Light rail, trams, guided light transit and guided buses are intended to move large numbers of people, swiftly and comfortably, along major traffic corridors within urban areas.

To be used the systems must be attractive to the passenger. To achieve this they must be perceived to be as efficient as the private car and in the same cost bracket in respect of the particular journey. They must also be environmentally acceptable, easily accessible, reasonably fast and comfortable, well-sited and sufficiently frequent, to be acceptable and desirable to potential passengers. Most users have a choice and they will exercise this according to whichever of the modes available to them for a particular journey offers the best 'value'.

Grenoble cars are equipped with plenty of hand-holds and a flat, low floor throughout the centre portion of the saloon.

Sheffield cars also have plenty of hand-grips colour-coded to show doorways and standee areas.

To achieve these purposes, and to be economically viable, large vehicles are used with passenger capacities sometimes in excess of two hundred. Electric power makes them quiet, gives good acceleration and braking qualities (and hence reasonably high service speeds) and does not pollute the atmosphere at the point of use.

To achieve accessibility large doors are fitted whilst well-designed interiors, large windows, decent seating and comfortable ride characteristics contribute to the impression of quality.

The system must also be operable safely and efficiently, provide adequate information and marketing services and be useable at reasonable cost.

There are benefits for non-users as well. Streets are less congested, there are fewer accidents, the air is cleaner and noise is reduced.

In order to be inserted easily into existing urban landscapes light rail is capable of tackling gradients greater than 1 in 10 and curves down to 25 metre radius (less for street-running tramways). The civil engineering required for bridges, embankments, tunnels and viaducts is reduced and what is necessary can be lighter and less intrusive than those for either road or railway.

There is not, however, one type of system or vehicle which can provide all the required and desirable benefits across the entire range of applications. A spectrum of modes has developed around the theme of transit provision, each with its own purpose and limitations, although with some measure of overlap. Some are based

The regional S-bahn in Bonn provides high speed limited stop services to outlying centres. Although it uses similar light rail vehicles to street tramways it is fully signalled and operates as heavy rail.

The Lille (France) system operates as a tramway throughout and includes both street running and reserved track operation.

on steel wheels on rails, others on pneumatic tyres either on guideways or the street. Some operate on reserved track, others share road space. Some are electrically powered, some by diesel engines, some by both. For certain applications even water power and gravity are applicable.

The Spectrum, Light Rail and Trams.

Electric light rail is a suitable mode for urban transport corridors carrying between about ten and twenty thousand passengers per hour in each direction. To achieve the higher numbers it needs to be segregated from other traffic. Light rail can be used virtually as a 'metro' system, express lines with limited stops over relatively long distances linking major urban centres with their satellite towns. This type of application is much used in Germany where it is referred to as an 'S-bahn'. Alternatively it can be applied to purely urban situations, providing transport through densely used areas within a city. Trams, modern versions of which are indistinguishable from light rail vehicles, operate largely at street level, either on reserved track in the roads median strip or alongside it. They can also operate through pedestrianised areas and in the street itself alongside other road vehicles. Their potential capacity per hour is roughly the same as for light rail but may be reduced where stops are more closely spaced and traffic conditions reduce service speeds.

Docklands Light Railway was originally intended to have a street-running section but this was abandoned in favour of a purely segregated system including the use of viaducts and in tunnel. It has been built as an automated, steel-wheel railway carrying no drivers and operated using a 'moving block' signalling system. On

Light rail provides a link between Berne and the satellite town of Worb. The tracks do not penetrate the city centre but terminate at Helvetiaplatz.

The interurban OEG system links Heidleberg with Mannheim (Germany).

Grenoble's system (above) is the benchmark against which others tend to be judged.

Street-running in Marseilles (right).

most railways, the line is divided into blocks (or sections) and only one train at a time is allowed into each. The moving block is a safety envelope, which can vary according to such parameters as traffic speed, based on each car. This enables closer headways, therefore more vehicles on a given section of track and allows a higher passenger capacity.

The Tyne and Wear Metro, the first of the new generation of light railways to be built in the UK, is also completely segregated. This system has drivers and is operated rather like a conventional railway.

Whilst all these kinds of systems are applicable to urban applications, light rail can also fulfil an 'inter-urban' role. Smaller cities with defined suburbs can benefit from this without the need for a complex, heavy-rail network. The line from Berne (Switzerland) to Worb is an example. Heidelberg is linked to Mannheim by light rail and the Ruhr valley has a broad network of 'inter-urban' lines between its many centres of population. Many of these centres also possess their own tramway systems. Towns along the Belgian coast are linked by tram. Light rail also plays a part in rural areas and for transport to defined tourist destinations. A number of rack and adhesion lines exist throughout Europe, including the Swiss and French Alps, where the ability to cope with steep gradients and sharp curves is of great benefit.

In areas of relatively low population density, or with a number of small centres, light rail can still have an application using diesel driven vehicles instead of electricity. This saves the cost of power generation, the provision and maintenance of an overhead current supply. Trams

Tram stops in Grenoble (above) and Strasbourg (below) with ticket machines, route maps and television monitors to provide information and waiting times.

French tramway warning signs (above) illustrate a rather more elegant car than their British counterparts (right).

propelled by internal combustion engines are not new. Belgium, for example, once had an extensive network of such lines. An example remains at Han sur Lesse where a tourist line to the nearby grotto is worked with original vehicles. The German tram and light rail vehicle builders, Duewag, have introduced a new diesel design using advanced techniques and a body shell drawn from electric practice. This is intended for lightly used 'inter-urban' lines.

Internal combustion-engined trams are also used in other places where electric power would be either too expensive or otherwise inappropriate. A number of pier tramways have used this source of power and a new line has been completed at Blackpool's North Pier. Generally, though, such applications are powered by electricity.

There is a growing movement to reintroduce early trams, suitably restored, into urban use as 'heritage tramways'. These are also intended to serve a conventional transport purpose within their urban areas. The system in Christchurch (New Zealand) is an example. 'Heritage' type cars, built recently, have been put into service elsewhere. The use of trams or tram-type vehicles is common for tourist routes, some examples have already been mentioned. There are, of course, a number of tramways which possess such cars but have a continuous history. Volk's Electric Railway is in this category, serving a tourist market for over a century. Traditional-type trams also operate on a line between Seaton and Colyton in Devon. In addition to electric motors and internal combustion engines, efforts have been made to produce a drive system which avoids both the cost and visual intrusion of overhead wires and the fumes of diesels.

Tram stop in Sheffield. Ticket machines, route panels and validators but no means of up-dating information.

Docklands car ascending towards Canary Wharf. Light rail can cope with steeper gradients and sharper curves than conventional railways.

Because of its flexibility light rail and tramways can be inserted into existing street patterns.

The most promising of these is the use of a fly-wheel mounted beneath the vehicle floor. The flywheel is brought to speed by an electric motor which collects current from a short conductor beneath the edge of each stopping-place platform. The flywheel stores this energy and drives the wheels through a constant-mesh, automatically variable gearbox, The system is intended for places, such as historic town centres and shopping precincts, where a traditional-looking vehicle is desirable. It is also thought to have application in less developed areas where costs are restricted.

People Movers.

Whilst the flywheel tram is referred to as a 'people mover', the term is usually applied to segregated systems using concrete guideways. In the UK these are mainly used to transport people over relatively short distances within an establishment where distances are too great to comfortably walk but open access is not desirable, such as at airports.

The people-movers (there are two separate lines) at Gatwick airport (London) were built by AEG Westinghouse and ride on pneumatic tyres on concrete track. Electric power is supplied via a rail between the wheels. The vehicles are guided by horizontally mounted wheels and are automatically driven. One line links the North and South terminals and possesses a continuous platform between the tracks. The terminus platforms are enclosed, doors along the walled platform edge line up with those on the vehicle and allow boarding once passengers have left through the doors on the other side. There are many similar systems worldwide.

Automatic, pneumatic-tyred people mover operated along concrete track at Gatwick Airport.

People mover interior. Arrows indicate exit side, seating is minimal and basic and there is, of course, no cab.

The VAL system in Lille (France) operates on the same principal as the people mover but is used to provide public transport services in the city.

As an alternative to 'metros' in France, a basically similar system of pneumatic-tyred, driverless vehicles running on guideways has been developed. Known as the VAL, Lille was the first centre to use them. They have now been in service for nearly a decade.

France has a tradition of innovation in urban transport, the first omnibuses and a range of differently powered street tramways were first tried there. The Paris Metro was the first to use pneumatic-tyred vehicles on a system which otherwise resembled a heavy-rail subway. Rubber-tyred, light metros are a feature of a number of French cities including Lyon and Marseilles. People-movers were proposed for a circular service in Southampton but fell to political action. Beyond the applications described above they have to compete with more traditional forms and have yet to acquire general acceptance.

Gatwick's other people mover uses single cars to serve the general aviation terminal.

Monorails.

There are two basically different types of monorail; one being suspended from an overhead track, the other straddling a guide and support beam. Both types are in service. The earliest extant system is the suspended Wuppertal monorail in Germany.

The straddle type is more common, although still rare. Von Roll, now part of AEG Westinghouse, developed a series of similar systems for a range of applications and load intensity. The Sydney circular line was built by them and there are several others in various parts of the world serving such places as hotels, entertainment complexes, theme parks and shopping malls where they provide transport between the centre and the car parks.

Parry 'Peoplemover' with a modern style body.

Such a system was built to serve the Merry Hill Shopping Centre in the West Midlands but is currently (1997) not operational. Another line is operated at Alton Towers theme park and a simpler, circular, scenic line operates at Beaulieu in Hampshire. Such systems have recently been utilised for transport within World Fair and Expo sites.

Suspended monorails either have wheels running on the upper surface of the track and connected to the car roof with angled suspension arms or have wheels in pairs either side of the suspension arm running in a hollow beam track. Straddle types have pneumatic-tyred wheels, often beneath seats unless the vehicle is large enough for the floor to clear the running-gear, rolling on the guide beam upper surface. The trains are articulated and each section usually has separate doors with no communication to the adjacent carriage. Small wheels, mounted horizontally beneath the floor, guide the vehicle along the beam. Power is collected by shoes running along a conductor strip.

Monorails have a powerful fascination due largely to their futuristic shape and can run above streets and their traffic, through buildings and across rivers and railway lines without extra bridge construction. They are, however, above the ground, necessitating lifts or escalators at all stops and careful station design, usually with automatic doors at each end of the platform track for safety reasons.

Except for very specific applications, monorails, like people movers, are in competition for construction with more conventional modes.

The monorail in Wuppertal (Germany) has been in service since the turn of the century. Cars are suspended beneath the track which, except at its western extremity, is constructed mainly over the river.

Train leaving station on the Merry Hill straddle monorail. The stations have automatic doors to close off the track exits.

Magnetic Levitation.

For eleven years until 1995, Birmingham Airport (UK) was served from the International railway station by a 'Maglev' system. This consisted of single cars operating along a concrete guideway. The car was suspended above the 'running rails' by the repelling force of a series of electromagnets. Propulsion was by linear induction motor.

The Maglev shuttle serving Birmingham's (West Midlands) International Station and airport is not currently in service.

Although few moving parts are involved, overall costs of these systems throughout their working lives are relatively high. Development costs have to be spread over very few systems, whilst maintenance and the cost of replacement parts, which may need to be specially manufactured, steadily increase. Revenue recovery was non-existent in the Birmingham case as the system was operated on a courtesy basis. The system may be replaced with a people-mover.

Guided Light Transit.

GLT is intended to gain the best from both bus and light rail. It is intended to run in the street, has both electric and diesel propulsion and can operate both on a guideway or be steered, using all wheels.

Articulated vehicles on three or more axles are used. In main traffic corridors they collect current, via a pantograph, from an overhead conductor. The current is earthed through a steel guideway in the road which also serves to steer the vehicle through its usual mechanism. Away from the guideway the pantograph and guide bogie are retracted, the diesel generator started and the vehicle may then be operated as a conventional, albeit rather large, bus.

Trolleybuses, this one in Marseilles, France, provide the benefits of electric traction whilst using ordinary road surfaces.

The concept is to provide a vehicle which, by being capable of use beyond the limit of the track, can provide transport from city centre to the edges of the suburbs without changing modes. The cost of such vehicles requires that they spend much of their time serving well-frequented corridors. They may not be so effective carrying a limited number of people around outlying housing estates. The Belgian manufacturer BN, now a division of the Bombardier Group, is the leader in this field. The installation of GLT is claimed to cost approximately 30% of an equivalent light rail system to build and to have similar operating characteristics. At the present time there are no public services operating this system although it has been considered in a number of cases.

Guided Buses.

The idea of guided buses, as opposed to bus lanes, is to decrease the headway between vehicles safely, thus enabling them to carry a greater passenger load, as a system, per hour. By using existing, and relatively inexpensive, technology it is argued that adequate public transport can be supplied at a substantial reduction on the cost of a completely new system. In Germany they are referred to as 'O-bahn'.

The buses are, in themselves, quite conventional except that they possess a set of horizontal guide-wheels in front of the leading road wheels. These engage between the 'kerbs' of the guideway and are linked to the buses steering. The guideway has a 'bell-mouth' approach so that the driver can cease steering once the

Guided buses - O-bahn - can operate as normal, diesel powered, wheel steered vehicles in the street. On their own reserved track they are self steered, guided by the horizontal guide wheels visible in the picture below.

The Essen (Germany) system will use electrical power on the guideways and certain other areas.

vehicle has entered it. Beyond the guideway the bus can be driven as normal. Experience with trials took place in the West Midlands but only in two places in the world have such systems been adopted. Apart from the fact that diesel fumes are still given out, such a system cannot carry the same volume of traffic per hour as light rail or trams. Additionally each vehicle must have a driver. Thus there is at least one crew member for every hundred passengers, more than twice the requirement for tracked vehicles. The track which guides these buses is a fairly massive, concrete construction making crossing by other traffic effectively impossible without resorting to a bridge or underpass. Experimental work on vehicles guided by underground wires is being carried out. This will remove the physical obstacles to cross traffic.

Cable cars at Matlock Bath (Derbyshire) linking the railway station with the Heights of Abraham.

Funiculars and Cable Cars.

These systems can only rarely be regarded as mass transit. They do, though, serve very specific functions and in places such as Lisbon (Portugal) funiculars form an integral part of the transport system.

A funicular railway is one in which the cars are linked via a cable to which they are permanently attached. They are used where the slope to be climbed is too steep for adhesion or rack rails. The angle of climb is always less than 1 in 1, so they are not technically lifts. The ascending car (or cabin) is helped by the force of gravity acting on the descending one. The necessary weight differential can be supplied by taking on water (as at Machynlleth and Lynton) or by mechanical means such as an electric motor as at most other sites.

The Bastille at Grenoble is linked to the town across the River Drac by this telepherique.

The tramway which climbs the Great Orme in Gwynedd is a street funicular; another operates at Shipley Glen in Bradford. The most usual application for funiculars in the UK is a means of access to the beach from a cliff top. The only urban funicular in the UK is at Bridgenorth (Shropshire), although there are others in Europe. The funicular at Le Havre has recently been refurbished and runs on pneumatic tyres on steel channel track. It is considerably longer than any in the UK. Funiculars are driven from the winding house but may carry a guard. Where the car is not permanently linked to the cable it is not a funicular but a cable-car. Probably the most famous of these are those in San Francisco (California). An endless cable in a conduit beneath the road is gripped by a set of jaws linked to the car. These jaws may be opened and closed by the driver. The cable moves at a continuous and steady speed. The jaws are released to stop, closed to restart.

Cable tramways were once more common. There were systems in Matlock and Edinburgh. The latter of these was electrified whilst the former closed down.

Another use of the term 'cable car' is to describe the cabins suspended from an endless cableway and usually associated with mountains. Although they are often used in hilly urban environments to link tourism sites or view points (as at Grenoble, France, Freiburg im Bresgau, Germany, and Mattock Bath, UK) they are not normally part of the settlement's mass transit system.

A different form of cable car - in fact a funicular railway - operates between Llandudno and the top of the Great Orme.

The Le Havre (France) electric funicular.

Moving walkways at Gatwick Airport.

One of Bournemouth's (Dorset) three electric cliff funiculars.

The funicular linking Lynmouth and Lynton uses hydraulic power.

The Seaton and District Tramway links the town of Seaton with Colyford and Colyton in Devon.

Left; Internal combustion engined trams used to operate on Ryde pier alongside steam trains to other island towns. These have now been replaced by re-used London tube stock on the one surviving route. These may, in turn, eventually be replaced by suitable light rail vehicles.

Rural and tourism services also benefit from light rail. This is the passing point on the electric, rack railway between Chamonix and the Mer du Glace in the French Alps.

Light rail may help in retaining the viability of threatened railways such as the Cambrian Coast Line.

The metre-gauge Palma to Inca (Majorca) line is served by diesel vehicles bearing many light rail characteristics.

Tramstop at Basle Bahnhof.

A view from the other side. The interior of a Berne low-floor car.

LIGHT RAIL AND GUIDED TRANSIT.

Section 4.

Finance, Consultation and Construction.

The systems outlined so far are parts of a broad range of guided transport modes which may be applied to resolving many of the increasing public transportation difficulties encountered in urban areas.

Before they can be operated, systems must be conceived, developed, financed, designed and built. New systems of any mode are expensive. To ensure that they represent value for the investment, the right tool for the job must be selected. The initial proposal may come from the local authority, either of its own initiative or as a result of suggestion from the private sector. The period between publication of the proposal and the commencement of operations may be several years, even decades. The time will have been filled with consultation, enquiry, development and design, acquisition of finance, tendering, marketing and construction. The process is fraught with pitfalls at any one of which the project may stall.

With the first generation tramways, the whole process was often handled by the local authority who became the proprietors and operators. There were also a number of commercial concerns which undertook the process on behalf of local authorities or as private ventures. A number of tramways in Africa were operated by Belgian undertakings. British Electric Traction built and operated several tramways in the UK.

Public consultation documents for proposed public transport projects in Leeds, Nottingham and the Vale of Severn.

81

In South America some systems were completely designed, constructed and equipped by British companies and then handed over to the local authority to operate.

Finance.

New systems are rarely developed by any single organisation. The finance comes from a range of sources including both the public and private sectors and the process is convoluted and confusing. Contracts may be let to design, build, operate and maintain; to design, finance and build or any combination. Those tendering for a contract may include consultants, civil engineers, vehicle manufacturers and operators of different transport systems from other areas. The grouping may only exist for the purposes of the one project. New construction and operation has now been going on for long enough for some companies to have acquired a great deal of experience in their fields. This reduces the need to 're-invent the wheel' for each project.

There are dramatically different approaches to the process in different parts of the world and variations between new building and extending existing systems.

Europe.

In Europe much of the funding for new schemes comes from central, regional or local government sources. Where appropriate, funds from the European Union may be available, especially where schemes are proposed for development areas.

The Centro project (W. Midlands) was delayed for many years due to government indecision over funding. The Strathclyde project was withdrawn for much the same reason.

Delta junction on the Docklands Light Railway, carrying lines to and from Tower Gateway/Bank, Stratford and Island Gardens via Canary Wharf. Light rail's flexibility is fully utilised.

The level and source of public funding varies from country to country as do the elements of the project for which it is intended. In Germany, grants amounting to around 85% of the infrastructure costs come from central sources (60%) and regional sources (25%). The remaining 15% is funded by either the city or the transport company itself who also meet all the costs for the rolling stock.

New systems in France are 50% funded by grants from central government. The remainder is met by the local authority. A transport tax is levied on all companies employing nine or more people within the authority's area. The level is set by the authority but the tax is raised centrally and paid to the authority.

A number of new systems in Spain and Italy have been funded in part by regional development grants as well as national and regional authorities. Funding may also be channelled through such bodies as the state railway where the system replaces their services. There is a range of variations on this theme. With the exception of the operator (if it is a private concern) and the transport tax, no private sector input is required.

Where new lines or upgrading takes place within an existing system the cost is met by the operators and their financial backers in nearly all cases.

The United States.

In the United States, funding may come via federal, state or local grants. Federal grants are allocated for 'transportation', rather than for roads, rail or other specified areas. In theory this

Grenoble (top), St. Etienne (middle) and Nantes (bottom) systems, owned by their respective local authorities, are operated by the private company Transcept.

allows long-term developments, such as light-rail systems, to be implemented without central interference. Once the decision has been made by the state, the funding process can begin. In practise the political nature of such decisions allows partially implemented programmes to be starved of funding if the controlling party changes during the construction period.

Local sales taxes may be raised to help fund new systems by complementing grants. These taxes, usually below 2%, may be applied by the state and the proceeds passed on to the transit authority. Transit authorities are responsible for all aspects of local public transportation within their districts. They may generate the initiative for new developments. As in Europe, once a system is constructed, the maintenance, repair and extension is largely the responsibility of the operators.

The United Kingdom.

Until 1993 all new systems proposed in the UK required either an Act of Parliament in order to proceed or were authorised under the terms of the Light Railways Act of 1896. They also had to comply, if they involved street running, with the Tramways Act of 1870. Since 1993 they may be authorised under the terms of the Transport and Works Act.

Government funds may be provided under Section 56 of the Transport Act of 1968. The decision is the Minister's who *'may with the approval of the Treasury make grants upon such terms and conditions as the Minister thinks fit to any person towards expenditure appearing to the Minister to be of a capital nature incurred or to*

Edinburgh and South-east Hampshire are two other areas hoping to resolve congestion and provide long-term environmental enhancement by providing car users with a viable and practical alternative. The Hampshire proposal involves a line linking Fareham with Portsmouth via Gosport and a tunnel under Portsmouth Harbour near the entrance.

be incurred by that person for the purpose of the provision, improvement or development of facilities for public passenger transport in Great Britain'. By the same section, local authorities may also provide grants if the scheme is seen as beneficial to their areas.

Movement towards the inclusion of 'private' capital in the development of transport schemes, Britain being the only country where a substantial level is required, has led to this being a condition before grants become available. There are three main sources of private capital; loans against expected operating profit, injections from contractors in the expectation of profit on the contracts and capital relating to enhanced property and site values along the route.

Manchester's trams are operated by Metrolink on behalf of the Passenger Transport Executive but are in competition with numerous private bus operators.

Government grants are also only available against the provision of non-user benefits. User benefits are seen as being the responsibility of the user for payment. Central grants under Section 56 of the Act must also be matched pound for pound by locally raised capital.

The non-user benefits which must be quantified include journey transfers from cars to the new system, reductions in road traffic volume together with road vehicle operating and road building costs, and cost reductions with regard to road accidents. These must be evaluated prior to grants becoming available, hence long before the system is built, let alone in use.

This has led to a situation where a great deal of effort has to be expended to develop means by which such potential benefits may be demonstrated in financial terms. Once agreed, it is quite feasible for the conditions to be altered as the

Sheffield's trams are operated by South Yorkshire Supertram Ltd. and are also in competition with local bus operators.

project progresses. The net result is a protracted and expensive process, which may fail to gain authorisation, be held up at any stage or dramatically amended as it progresses.

There are examples of proposals being approved by the local authority, partially funded and meeting the apparent criteria for grants, and then being refused authorisation and of authorised projects, with funding in place and Ministerial statements made in their favour, having the financial 'goal-posts' moved and being held up for years. It appears that, in the UK, the development of public transport for its own sake, that is the transportation of the public, receives a low priority on the part of government. However, a number of schemes have run the gauntlet more or less successfully. New systems have been constructed in Tyne and Wear, London Docklands, Manchester and Sheffield. A number of others, though, remain in abeyance awaiting grants or authorization.

New public transport projects are expensive whether they involve a new fleet of buses or a complex light rail network. The processes for authorization and funding are complicated and protracted.

Consultation.

Public consultation is a necessary feature of the process between proposal and construction in all cases where transportation systems require infrastructure or are radically different from the area's existing systems.

Once a project is commenced there remains a need to continue to provide information on benefits and progress.

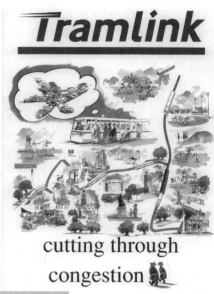

Consultation serves a number of purposes and may range from ascertaining perceptions and opinions regarding different types of mode of transport to views on specific aspects of proposed routes. The earliest stages of public consultation might include 'focus groups' to gather overall ideas on how people view new concepts. Later, views on the choice of system for the area might be investigated. The final stages of the process might involve consulting every individual and business along a proposed route. Aspects of consultation with the public in the UK include the considerations that many people have scant knowledge of guided transit systems and that a majority of those with knowledge or experience of travel on them will have acquired this in circumstances other than their usual day-to-day activities. Many will have seen or used such systems whilst on holiday or have seen them in the context of tourist attractions rather than transport tools. In addition, public perception of guided transit systems will be very different from that of professionals in the planning or transport fields.

Construction.

Construction of guided transit systems is invariably a major operation. The cost, time-scale and level of disruption will depend on many factors. These will include the type of system, the route, the amount of existing infrastructure to be used and the level of segregation. The selected route may be along the major traffic-flow corridors or may be designed to include development areas. Depending on the mode to be used, it may be entirely street-running, completely segregated (even entirely on viaduct) or

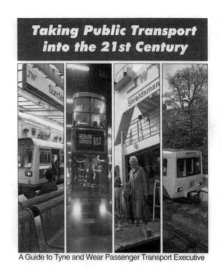

A Guide to Tyne and Wear Passenger Transport Executive

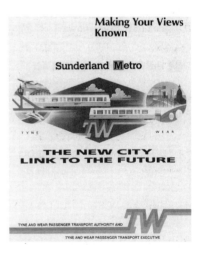

The Tyne and Wear Metro has been operating for many years. It continues to furnish progress information and consult on plans for extension and development.

any stage in between. One of the major elements of construction costs is the building of infrastructure such as bridges, embankments and tunnels. Where these already exist (for example on heavy rail lines which are no longer required and are appropriately sited) they are often re-used. Ideal routes may be amended to take advantage of these if possible.

Where tracked systems are to run in the street, all the underground services, such as gas, water, telephone conduits, sewers and so on, are moved to ensure that they are no longer directly beneath the right-of-way (except to cross it). Such systems are the most disruptive during construction but construction schedules are usually designed to minimise this. It is in the interests of the promoters to complete construction in the minimum practical time. In addition guided transit systems require lighter infrastructure than heavy rail projects. They are often quicker to build. The construction of a new transit system of any mode will involve some disruption unless it is being built in an environment as yet inaccessible to the public.

In some cases construction of a complete system will be undertaken in a single stage. Where a system is extensive, funding is only available in stages or construction depends on the completion of other projects, construction will take place in phases. Each phase may commence operation as it is completed. All existing light rail systems in the UK were constructed in stages. Further extensions are intended on several of them. An important aspect of new systems is that they must allow for future changes.

The imposing Canary Wharf station on the Docklands Light Railway serves as an interchange between the lines.

Docklands initial railway terminal at Island Gardens reflects local historic architecture.

Systems intended to operate within a 'closed' environment, such as a shopping centre or tourist attraction, are usually constructed in one phase, sometimes as part of the construction of the centre itself. It is an indication of the flexibility of the range of modes available that they may be added to existing environments with minimal disruption or designed-in from the beginning of a project.

G-Mex is where street running ceases and reserved track operation begins on the Manchester system.

Systems acquire their own histories and are often the subject of pride amongst their operators, workforces and the communities they serve. This is reflected in the publication of history books, 'operational handbooks' and postcards, for example. Anniversary events and associated publications are another feature.

Berne four-axle car and trailer in the city centre.
A classic tramway, the street is available only to
pedestrians and electric public transport.

LIGHT RAIL AND GUIDED TRANSIT.

Section 5. Operation.

Routes and Networks.

Route selection for both new systems and extensions of existing ones will be largely determined by transportation needs. Other factors, such as existing infrastructure, the desire to assist in the development of particular areas of a city and to produce the greatest level of change from private transport, will have 'tuning' effects on this.

Many of the first generation tramways were constructed to link centres within an urban area and were then extended out to the suburbs. In some cases the existence of a tramway generated suburban development. Further out, the suburbs were largely served by railways. In many cases present day bus services follow this pattern.

The present trend, in the case of new light rail schemes, is to provide one or more routes running out from the centre. This radial pattern serves the main transit corridors and allows for transfer at the centre. A single line may well serve outlying areas at opposite sides of the centre. Within the centre, different points can be linked providing 'city centre' services. A number of inbound routes can use the same track within the central area reducing the need for passenger transfer and ensuring a higher frequency of service. In Zurich, for example, a number of the city centre stops are served by up to six routes and nearly all are joined by at least two. Each of the two principal bridges is crossed by five routes.

The terminal building of Rouen's spur line to Sotteville makes statements about civic pride and permanence regardless of personal opinions regarding its architectural merit.

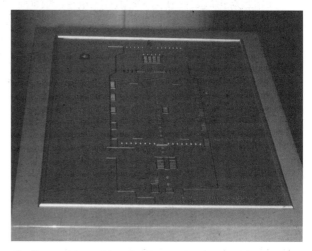

Brail station guides in Brussels (above) represent one way in which the system caters for the whole community.

Route maps and timetables are provided by all European systems. Some verge on being works of art.

The routes are arranged so that nearly all traffic centres have at least one alternative route to all the other centres. In some places in the city centre it is unnecessary to consult a timetable as the service is so frequent.

Similar route structures may be found in a number of European cities, all of which have possessed tramways for many years. Brussels, Vienna, Lisbon, Cologne, Hanover, Munich, Basle and Dresden are some of the many possessing intensive radial routes.

A feature of some of these, notably Vienna, is that the radial arms join a central ring or loop which carries all the routes close to the central district.

Radial networks consist, essentially, of a number of single routes meeting at the centre. There are many systems with few routes and several with only one. Linear routes can serve two outlying districts, linking them through the urban centre as is the case in Manchester. They may also provide a link between centres of adjacent towns. The Belgian coastal line passing through Ostend is a well-known example of this.

Many of the historically continuous systems rely heavily on street running. In a number of cases this has been improved by traffic reduction or pedestrianisation on sections of route and by constructing tracks on reservations either at the side of the road or, on dual-carriageways, in the centre. Under these circumstances it is unnecessary to pave the track which can be laid on ballast. For aesthetic reasons, though, many systems grass the track.

The terminal of the Line 12 in Geneva is very close to the French frontier. The buildings in the background are, in fact, in France. The border post is about fifty metres down the road from the simple terminal building. Basle also has routes terminating within sight of another country.

Six of Zurich's cross-city routes pass via the Bahnhoffstrasse. To travel within the central district it is not necessary to consult a timetable.

Reserved track may improve journey times but intersections still have to be crossed 'at grade'. Priority signalling can ameliorate problems in this area and street or reserved track at street level makes for immediate access and keeps the trams in view.

Segregated track, either in tunnel, on viaduct or at grade on separate right-of-way (like railways), improves journey times even more and allows the system to operate in its own right without concern for other road users. Such an approach is more expensive and often less accessible as well as creating an impression of a separate system, not linked in any way with other traffic. Stations are often further apart than on systems associated with the street, serving areas rather than specific places.

Pre-existing railway infrastructure is used where possible to save construction costs and also because the right-of-way is already established. The lines themselves are free of other traffic. Track sharing is becoming an option in some cases where the volume of heavy rail traffic is light. Karlsruhe has successfully experimented with this idea, overcoming many of the reservations expressed, especially about safety. This approach is now being considered elsewhere.

Guided light transit, requiring a single guide rail, is as flexible as street tramways regarding major traffic corridors. An advantage is claimed in that, at the outer ends of the main sections of route, the vehicle can convert from guided / electric to driver steered / diesel and continue beyond the end of the track, avoiding the need for passengers to transfer from one vehicle to another.

Trams and trolleybuses share the stands outside Berne's Hauptbahnhof.

Reserved track climbing out of Sheffield city centre.

Approaching Island Gardens on reserved track using existing railway viaducts, Docklands.

There are no such systems in revenue operation at the present date and therefore no data on the economic viability of operating expensive, dual system, articulated vehicles at the low passenger levels likely at route extremities. For the same reason no long-term evidence exists for their practicality on the restricted streets of the suburbs. There is no doubt that such systems will have a place in the spectrum, possibly as a main-corridor mover between buses and light rail in passenger capacity.

Guided buses possess the same advantage as GLT but remain diesel-powered all the time and lack the carrying capacity of other systems. The guideways preclude sharing with other traffic. Such systems must be segregated as crossing the guideways at grade is impossible. This reduces the on-street accessibility of the mode and adds to the cost. Although buses using the guideways could operate at higher frequency, they still would not match the capacity of rail guided systems.

In terms of capabilities to meet the requirements of urban space, the different modes have much in common. All can tackle curves down to around eighteen metre radius (i.e. they can go round street corners) and climb grades of about eight per cent. Where they differ, apart from the nature of their guide tracks, is in their carrying capacity, useful life expectancy and staff operating costs.

Whilst guided transit systems are very flexible in that they can be inserted into existing environments in a variety of ways, they cannot, for engineering as well as economic reasons, be built to serve every street. They need, therefore, to be fed.

Karlsruhe has dual-voltage trams capable of operating on both street track and DB railway lines. Older cars in its fleet are in the process of being replaced.

Tram and bus with a common terminus at La Terrasse, St. Etienne. The tram traverses the city centre whilst buses provide onward conveyance into the suburbs.

Park and ride is a common feature of such systems, often with the parking ticket covering use of the transit system. Where the system is part of a commonly-owned, urban transport operation the bus routes can be organised to provide feeder services throughout the suburbs and to link the spokes of the network as well as providing supporting services in the centre. This is a usual feature in Europe but is not the case in the UK, where transport has been deregulated.

Headway and Frequency.

For any system to be used, especially if it is to be seen as a viable alternative to the car, it must provide transport when and where the user requires. Services need to be frequent, reliable, constant in journey time and extended over a great part of the day.

Headway, the time between vehicles on a particular service, is an important consideration as its maintenance indicates that the system is functioning properly and regularly. Frequency, the number of vehicles on a particular service passing a certain spot in a given time, is not such a reliable guide. Twenty vehicles per hour is not attractive if they arrive in two bunches separated by forty five minutes. The frequency would appear as twenty per hour but the headway, ostensibly three minutes, would, in fact be varying from three quarters of a minute to three quarters of an hour.

There is also a need to provide a greater intensity of service during 'rush hours' than during the remainder of the day. These are likely to be at the end of the evening as well as at the beginning and end of the business day.

Grand Union junction in Basle.

The workshops at Nunnery depot, Sheffield.

Track repairs in Basle without disrupting services.

Partly because of the cost of investment in vehicles and infrastructure, the variation throughout the day is likely to be relatively slight. In terms of costs, the power consumption is relatively light and the driver of a tram or light rail vehicle is in charge of a vehicle with up to three times the capacity of a bus. They are, essentially, too valuable to be left in the depot. Guided transit is therefore likely to provide a more constant service throughout the day.

To provide an integrated system buses can be used as feeders and the main routes should serve the principal railway stations and, if appropriate, airports and docks.

Carrying capacities (usually expressed in terms of passengers per hour per direction) vary amongst the modes and are a major consideration in deciding which is the most appropriate for a system.

As an example, consider a twenty kilometre, cross-town route to be served by either bus, street-running tram (with reserved track outside the centre) or segregated light rail.

To carry 1,000 passengers per hour per direction would require thirteen buses per hour (approximately a four and a half minute headway). To maintain the service would require a fleet of twenty nine buses on the road, with, of course, twenty nine drivers and, possibly, two travelling inspectors.

The conventional tramway would require five vehicles per hour (a twelve minute headway), ten to maintain the service, ten drivers and one inspector.

A range of marketing material produced by various European operators includes models in plastic and card.

For the benefit of visitors, a number of operators provide explanatory leaflets on how to use their systems.

Lille (France) provides a detailed guide to its system of bus, tram and automatic metros. The VAL is pneumatic-tyred, fully automatic people-mover.

Segregated light rail would require four vehicles per hour at a fifteen minute headway (two vehicles per hour if operated as a multiple unit half hour headway.) Seven vehicles could maintain the service, seven drivers and one inspector.

If passenger flow was 5,000 per hour the figures for the bus rise to over sixty per hour (less than one minute headway) with one hundred and thirty four vehicles being required to maintain the service. The tramway would need twenty five vehicles per hour (just under two and a half minutes headway) and fifty vehicles to maintain the service. Light rail would need twenty vehicles at three minute headway with thirty two being needed to cover the service (ten per hour and sixteen in total if worked as multiple units).

At 10,000 per hour, bus operation becomes impossible (the headway would be under half a minute and nearly three hundred vehicles would be needed to operate the service.) The tram system's headway would be one and a quarter minutes with around one hundred in operation. Light rail, in multiple unit operation, would be passing every three minutes with thirty two multiple units (or twice the number of single units) being needed to maintain the service.

It is not uncommon for trams and light rail systems to operate to these figures. Zurich endeavours to provide headways not exceeding six minutes and other systems offer frequencies greater than ten per hour. To maintain headways (and hence timetables) electronic tracking and updating systems are often employed. These keep the control room informed of the actual position of each vehicle and they, in turn advise the driver.

Southern terminus of the St. Etienne tramway.

Docklands cars awaiting service.

It is common to use the data to inform intending passengers of service status through video screens or moving light displays at stops.

Stops.

Stops are the part of the infrastructure which most affects the intending passenger. Guided transit stops vary from a simple sign on a pole to a complete station. Older systems may have a variety of designs reflecting what was thought appropriate at the time of their construction or extension. Termini may well include lavatories, snack bars and information kiosks.

New systems tend to have their stops constructed to a common style which reflects the modernity and efficiency of the mode, as well as shelter and seating, stops will also possess ticket machines, route and network information and, increasingly, constantly updated service status information to keep people informed of waiting times, next vehicle destinations and restrictions.

At some point on the system, often at stops serving main railway stations and entertainment or commercial centres, there is likely to be a staffed information centre which can provide service information, special tickets and a range of marketing goods such as postcards, handbooks and models. Marketing is an important aspect of system operation and most cities which possess them are proud of their systems and recognise the interest which they generate. Such marketing also provides revenue.

Tickets.

Tickets provide a number of purposes in addition to providing a permit to travel and a receipt

The end of route 12, Geneva, is close to the French frontier.

Tickets come in all shapes and sizes and a number of different materials. Some are 'journey-only', others allow travel for, say, up to an hour and a quarter, yet others all day - some for groups and on a number of linked systems. Tickets are rarely available on the vehicle in Europe, being bought from machines at the stops or from nearby shops acting as agencies.

for the fare. They enable the operator to monitor usage of the system, to chart passenger flows and to reconcile revenue receipts.

Few systems sell tickets on board the vehicle. This method would require either an additional crew member on each vehicle or occupy too much time at each stop if the driver were to sell them. To provide a reliable and swift service, boarding and disembarking must take place as rapidly as is comfortably possible thus minimising the dwell time at stops.

There is often a range of tickets available, more than simply adult and child, single or return. Many operators provide day or period tickets for visitors as well as season tickets for regular users. Tickets may be bought in batches at a discount or at a reduced price if purchased from agents rather than the machines at stops.

In Europe, and increasingly elsewhere, tickets are rarely for a distance but more often for a length of time, say one or one and a quarter hours after the time of validation. This enables changes and transfers to other modes to be made where all are under the same operator. Sometimes there are restrictions to prevent the return journey being made on the same ticket.

Tickets sold prior to boarding the vehicle require validation at the start of the journey. This is done by a machine which prints the time of validation, and starting point, on the ticket. These machines can be either on the vehicle or at the stop. It is always an offence to travel without a valid (and validated) ticket.

Inspection is usually on a random basis, often by teams who can cover all the doors. Inspectors are empowered to levy on-the-spot fines.

Textured surfaces on Sheffield's tramway platforms indicate where the doors will stop.

Station on the Merry Hill monorail. Tickets are purchased before entering the platform.

Terminus of Basle route 6 with cafe, kiosk and toilets.

The ticket machines themselves can sometimes supply updated information to the control centre electronically. Thus the operator has minute by minute monitoring of how the service is progressing, passenger flows, when additional ticket supplies are required or when machines need emptying. The tickets often have coding strips printed on them which can be read by validators or electronic gates. Thus journey types can be monitored.

In the UK, off-vehicle purchase is common to all the light rail and most of the tramway and other guided systems. Only Blackpool retains on-vehicle purchase, sold by the driver or, on double-deck cars, by a conductor. Nearly all bus services employ on-vehicle purchase. The range of tickets is often less extensive than in Europe and elsewhere and opportunities for transfer between modes are limited.

Beyond the City Limits.

Whilst guided transit is principally used in urban situations it is not exclusively so. Throughout Europe and the United States there were large numbers of inter-urban and rural tramways. Many of these have since disappeared but there remain examples between Berne and Worb in Switzerland and around Lille in France. Switzerland possesses a large number of electrically powered light railways serving outlying communities and tourist centres.

It is difficult to draw lines between the various modes, especially in the range described as light rail. Nevertheless their numbers are increasing; they have been shown to provide clean, efficient transport to a standard likely to persuade travellers to use them instead of cars and to enhance the urban environment. Light rail is

Ticket machines in Basle (above) and London Docklands (below).

much advanced from the trams so fondly remembered in the UK. It is not an anachronism but offers a realistic means of reducing pollution and congestion whilst improving the atmosphere and security of city centres.

The various modes which make up the spectrum of guided transit, together with buses and trolleybuses, all have their places in the various urban, commercial, transport and heritage centres which require transit facilities. There may be much more to be gained from integrating the modes into a coherent system than endeavouring to garner competition between types which have essentially different benefits and are intended for different purposes.

The diesel-powered Grottes de Hann tram (above) conveys passengers to the caves whilst the OEG (below) links Heidelberg with Mannheim.

Near Chamonix station on the line to the Mer de Glace.

Sheffield, Fitzalan Square. The upper picture was taken prior to the completion of the extension to Middlewood, the lower picture shows the same stop (from the opposite direction) after the extension was opened.

APPENDIX 1.

Operational Tramway and Light Rail Systems in the Mainland UK.

BLACKPOOL TRAMWAYS
Blackpool Borough Council Transport Department.

Coastal tramway between Fleetwood Ferry and Starr Gate, Blackpool. 18.5 kilometres, principally reserved track or on pedestrianised promenade, street running in Fleetwood and Talbot Square, Blackpool.

Commenced Operation:
September 1895 (Cocker St. to South Pier).
Present extent: 1902

Power supply: 560V D.C. overhead.

Rolling Stock: 65 four-axle cars of which 12 new since 1979. Various builders. 26 double-deck, remainder single deck, none articulated.

History: Opened on September 29th, 1895, the original 3 kilometre route was supplied with power via a conduit between the running rails. It was the first electrically powered street tramway in the United Kingdom.

In 1899, by which time the tramway had been extended considerably, it was converted to conventional, overhead current collection. Between 1895 and 1904 a number of routes away from the coast were developed (since closed) and the coastal tramway was moved from the street to the promenade in stages. In 1920 the Corporation bought the Blackpool and Fleetwood Tram-road Company and through running over the present route began. (Although the tracks had been there for 22 years, the two undertakings had no physical connection before this date.)

Many early vehicles were rebuilt during the Twenties and new cars bought in the Thirties (some of which, in turn rebuilt, are still in service). By the 1960s it had become necessary to consider the future of the operation, which by then was the last surviving traditional tramway in the country. Following experiments with hauled trailers, a major rebuilding programme involving over a dozen 1930s 'railcoaches' was carried out, converting them to one man operation. Two double deckers were also rebuilt in the late 1970s experimenting with various stair and door combinations for maximum efficiency and, again, for one man operation.

The rebuilt single deckers began to be replaced during the mid 1980s with what were essentially new cars using some of the equipment from earlier vehicles.

Like the 'new' double deckers, their appearance owes much to the bus body components used to reduce costs. The cost of each new vehicle is roughly half that of buying 'off-the-shelf' continental cars. The ten cars of this batch are sufficent to operate the basic winter service without augmentation.

The Future: Blackpool has recently taken the decision to retain its trams and modernise the infrastructure, although there are no plans for extensions. No longer the only light rail or tramway system in the country, it remains the oldest continuous serving undertaking.

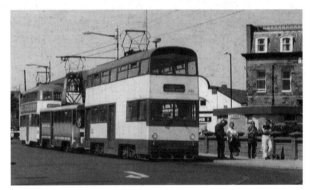

DOCKLANDS LIGHT RAILWAY.

Docklands Light Railway Ltd., P.O. Box 154, Poplar, E14 9QA.

Automatically controlled, fully segregated, urban light rail system. Based largely on pre-existing railway rights of way, it includes within its initial 12 km. approximately 4 km. of new construction with a further 1 km. (opened as a second stage) in tunnel. The initial system comprises three legs linked at Canary Wharf. 16 stations are served.

Commenced Operation: July 1987 (initial railway)
July 1991 (Bank extension)

Power Supply: 750V D.C., under-running third rail.

Rolling Stock: 80 six-axle, articulated, driverless cars in three batches; 10 P89 type by BREL, 23 P90 type by BN, 47 P92 type by BN.

History: Construction of the initial Docklands Light Railway was authorised in October 1982. It consisted of three 'legs', the railway going from Tower Gateway to the (then) station at West India Quay, where the route divided, one leg going to Stratford, the other going to Island Gardens on the Isle of Dogs, opposite Greenwich. The initial railway opened in July 1987 and was served by eleven automatic, driverless, articulated cars. These have since been sold to Essen in Germany.

The underground extension to Bank and the opening of Canary Wharf required major alterations to the operation of trains with both Bank and Tower Gateway as city termini and all trains going to Canary Wharf with an off-peak shuttle to Island Gardens. So great was the increase in passenger traffic that much station rebuilding was required to allow for two car trains.

Trains are protected by a 'moving block' signalling system in which trains travel within an 'envelope' which allows running on reduced headways, even coming up to each other, thus making more efficient use of track space.

The Future: A branch to Beckton, where the main depot has been constructed, and serving an additional twelve intermediate stations is awaiting opening. Plans are in preperation for a further extension across the River Thames to Lewisham. The present headway of eight minutes is expected to be halved at peak times on the existing railway.

Upper photos: Docklands Light Railway. Lower photo: Great Orme, upper section.

GREAT ORME TRAMWAY.

Grwp Aberconwy, Aberconwy Borough Council, Chapel Street, Llandudno, Gwynedd.

Funicular tramway operating over one and a half kilometres of street and reserved track between Victoria Station, Llandudno and the summit of the Great Orme. Both upper and lower sections are single track with passing loop and are served by cables driven from a central winding house. The steepest gradient is 1 in 3.9 on the lower section. Seasonal service.

Commenced operation:	July 1902.
Upper section;	July 1903.

Power supply: Original steam powered winding engines replaced with electric motors of 125 horse power (lower) and 75 horse power (upper).

Rolling stock: 4 four-axle, open platform cars (two per section) by Hurst Nelson.

History: Track layout has not altered since 1905 and original vehicles are still in use. Freight service (principally coal to the winding house) discontinued during 1930s. Steam machinery replaced by electric motors in 1958. Radio communication replaced telegraph system in 1990 but 'trolley poles' retained for appearance. Last surviving street, cable railway in the United Kingdom.

MANCHESTER METROLINK.

Greater Manchester Metro Ltd., Metrolink House, Queens Road, Cheetham Hill, Manchester, M8 7KY.

Urban light rail system operating between Bury and Altrincham via central Manchester and Piccadilly Station. Of 31 km. of route, just over 28 km. are on reserved (ex-railway) rights of way whilst the remainder are on street in the city centre. 26 stations and stops are served. Stops in the street are provided with dual-level platforms.

Commenced Operation:
April 6th 1992 (Bury to Victoria Street)
April 27th 1992 (Victoria to G-Mex)
June 15th 1992 (G-Mex to Altrincham)
July 27th 1992 (Piccadilly spur)

Power Supply:	750V D.C. overhead.
Rolling Stock:	26 six-axle, articulated cars by Firema Consortium.

History: The concept which became Metrolink developed over twenty years in response to growing congestion in central Manchester and the lack of a rail link across the city centre between the two major railway stations.

Approval was received in 1989. Construction was carried out by a consortium whose activities included all aspects of design, building, operation and maintenance under complex contracts to the Greater Manchester Passenger Transport Executive. Originally planned as part of an integrated, overall transport system, public transport deregulation prevented this from taking place. Funding came from the consortium itself, the Passenger Transport Authority and the Government (a grant under Section 56 of the 1968 Transport Act).

Upon completion of construction in 1992 it became the first street running tramway to operate in the U.K. (with the exception of Blackpool) for thirty years and the first to use new light rail technology.

Sunday working commenced in November 1992 and peak time multiple unit operation on 26th April 1993. Services operate on a six minute headway.

The Future: Proposals exist for extensions to Ashton-under-Lyne, Manchester Airport, Rochdale, Salford and Trafford Park. These would total an additional 35 km. of route and require around 30 new vehicles.

SEATON AND DISTRICT ELECTRIC TRAMWAY.
Harbour Road, Seaton, Devon.

Five kilometre, narrow-gauge line between Seaton and Colyton. The majority of the line follows the right-of-way of the now defunct Southern Railway Seaton Branch but has been extended to a new terminus near the centre of Seaton. Single track with passing loops, there is an intermediate stop at Colyford.

Commenced operation:
1971 (first passenger service)
Present extent: 1980 (to Colyton)
1995 (new terminus)

Power supply: 110V D.C. overhead.

Rolling stock: 9 bogie cars largely based on double deck originals and using parts from earlier cars Nos. 14 and 16 are enclosed single deckers whilst no. 17 is equipped to carry wheelchairs. All constructed by the operators.

History: Originally operated at Eastbourne, the company moved to its present location during 1970. First services were with a battery powered car. Operation to Colyford began in 1973 and to Colyton in 1970. The line from the depot (on the site of Seaton railway station) to the town runs around the various holiday camps and has recently been slightly extended to include a new, purpose built terminus.

The Future: The tramway has now reached its intended extent. Plans are in hand to rebuild an original Exeter car for operation.

SHEFFIELD SUPERTRAM.

South Yorkshire Supertram Ltd., 11 Arundel Gate, Sheffield, S1 2NP.

Urban light rail system centred on Sheffield with routes to Meadowhall, Middlewood/Malin Bridge and Halfway/Herdings Park comprising 30 route kilometres of which approximately half are on street. When the system is fully open 45 stops will be served.

Commenced Operation:
March 21st 1994 (Fitzalan Square to Meadowhall)
August 22nd 1994 (Fitzalan Square to Spring Lane)
Dec. 5th 1994 (Spring Lane to Gleadless Town End)
Feb. 18th 1995 (Fitzalan Square to Cathedral)
Feb. 27th 1995 (Cathedral to Shalesmoor)

Power Supply: 750V D.C. overhead.

Rolling Stock: 25 eight-axle, three section, low floor, articulated cars by Siemens-Duewag. All axles are powered.

History: Following the final closure of the first-generation tramway in October 1960, Sheffield began to suffer the common problems caused by expansion of traffic volumes. From 1972 a series of studies considerd the transport need of the city in the (then) future culminating in a detailed review in 1982 which led to the decision in principle to construct a modern light rail system. A bill was placed before Parliament in 1985.

After resolution of objections, the Act was passed in 1988 with a further Act in 1989 enabling further lines. Construction of the first of eight planned phases (Meadowhall Line) began in August 1991 and the route opened in 1994. Construction continues on the outstanding phases which are anticipated for completion during 1996.

Upper left photo: Seaton.
Left and far left: Sheffield.

TYNE AND WEAR METRO.

Tyne and Wear Passenger Transport Executive, Cuthbert House, All Saints, Newcastle-upon-Tyne, NE1 2DA.

Urban, light rail 'metro' system. 55 kilometres of fully segregated right of way including 13 km. of new construction and 5 km. in tunnel. The system comprises four routes radiating from Monument Station (underground) in the city centre. Outlying termini include South Shields and Newcastle Airport. There are 46 stations of which 26 serve more than one route.

Commenced Operation:
1980 (Haymarket to Tynemouth)
1984 (remainder of 1973 authorisation)
1992 (airport extension)
Power Supply: 1,500v D.C. overhead

Rolling Stock: 90 six-axle, articulated cars by Metro Cammell (based on Stadtbahn B cars).

History: Parliamentary authorisation was received in 1973 following the Tyne and Wear Plan of 1971 which recommended a new urban railway as the pivot of a fully integrated public transport system.

Work commenced in 1974 and the first section - between Haymarket and Tynemouth - opened in 1980. Further sections under the original authorisation were opened progressively until, by 1984, the basic system was complete. Monument Station, through which all four routes operate (the St. James to Pelaw route twice) is the focus of the system.

An extension to Newcastle International Airport was authorised in 1990 and opened in 1992.

As a comprehensively designed system with potential for extension, both stations and vehicles have been designed for ease of access for able-bodied, encumbered and disabled passengers. Tyne and Wear Metro is the first modern light rail system in the United Kingdom.

The Future: It is planned to extend to the south bringing Washington and Sunderland into the system when a satisfactory route can be agreed. The system currently operates double cars at an average of 3.5 minute headway at peaks, giving a capacity of 7,000 passengers per hour. It is possible to more than double this within the existing infrastructure.

VOLK'S ELECTRIC RAILWAY.

Resort Services Department, Brighton Borough Council, Brighton, East Sussex.

Two kilometre coastal line between Brighton Aquarium and Black Rock (Marina). Single track with passing loops, one intermediate station only. 40 seat, two-axle cars normally operated in pairs. Seasonal service.

Commenced operation:	August 1883
Reopened western section;	April 1884
Present extent;	May 1902

Power supply: 125V D.C. Third rail.

Rolling stock: 9 two-axle, partly enclosed cars varying in date from 1892 to 1926.

History: First public, electric railway in the United Kingdom opened on August 4th 1883 with a one third kilometre track extending eastwards from the Palace Pier. In the following year it was extended to Banjo Groyne and, in 1902, to Black Rock. Both ends of this route have subsequently been cut back by about one quarter kilometre.

Originally a 'two rail' system, both extensions were built with a third conductor rail. When first constructed, most of the route was on viaduct level with the promenade, but the beach has subsequently built up so that is now at grade.

Following a period of uncertainty during the 1960s, when traffic fell considerably, the railway was largely rebuilt in 1990 -1991. The basic service is at 15 minute headway in each direction with supplementaries at peaks.

The future: Although there are no firm plans the line may be re-extended to the Palace Pier and possibly into the Marina. A 'friends' organisation assists with operation.

APPENDIX 2.

Other Operational Guided Transit Systems in the Mainland UK.

GATWICK AIRPORT (1); Automatic people-mover between North and South terminals. Twin concrete tracks with continuous service platform and guide rail. Pneumatic tyred. AEG C100, three car units. Enclosed entrance platforms at each terminus with sliding doors matched to the vehicle. 'Tidal-flow' access system.

GATWICK AIRPORT (2); Automatic people-mover between North and General Aviation terminals. As main system (to which it is not linked) but using single, AEG C50 cars.

BIRMINGHAM AIRPORT; Maglev (magnetic levitation) people-mover between Birmingham International railway station and the airport passenger terminal. This system is not currently operational and may be replaced by a more conventional system.

WEST MIDLANDS MERRY HILL CENTRE; AEG (Von Roll) straddle-type monorail between Merry Hill business park and the shopping mall. Includes four stations three of which are within the retail precinct. Multiple car trains. Double track with depot close to business park terminal. This system is not currently operational.

The two separate people movers at Gatwick Airport (above between the main terminals, below to the general aviation terminal).

Maglev linking Birmingham Airport and station.

Straddle monorail at Merry Hill (W. Midlands). Neither system is currently operational.

Pier Tramways.

BLACKPOOL, NORTH PIER; Narrow-gauge, double track, diesel tramway. Track length 250 metres. Opened 1991.

HYTHE PIER (HAMPSHIRE); Narrow-gauge, single track tramway operated in conjunction with Hythe - Southampton ferries. Electric locomotive hauled, the locomotive serving originally in a munitions factory.

SOUTHEND PIER; Electric, double track between North and South (for pier head) stations. Originally opened in 1890, the present system commenced operation in 1986. Track length 1,200 metres. An exhibition concerning the development of the pier and its railway is housed beneath the North station.

Electric locomotive on the Hythe Pier tramway on Southampton Water.

Diesel powered tram on Blackpool's North Pier tramway.

Public Park Tramways.

BRADFORD, SHIPLEY GLEN CABLE TRAMWAY;
Narrow gauge, funicular tramway close to Saltaire, Yorks. Operates four-wheeled, open, toastrack cars with trailers controlled by a tramway controller at the upper station. Track length 350 metres. Opened 1895. A museum is in the course of development.

CARDIFF, HEATH PARK TRAMWAY; Miniature tramway operating on Sundays and Bank Holidays only. Track length 300 metres.

MANCHESTER, HEATON PARK TRAMWAY; Standard gauge tramway operating cars from Blackpool and Manchester. Small museum. Track length 750 metres.

WALSALL, ARBORETUM PARK; Miniature tramway operating on Sundays only. Track length 700 metres.

Top Right: The cable tramway at Shipley Glen.

Above and Right: The tramway and museum at Heaton Park, Manchester.

Funicular Railways and Cliff Lifts.

ABERYSTWYTH, CONSTITUTION HILL FUNICULAR;
At north end of Promenade, links with camera obscura and cliff walks from top station. Stepped, open, cross-bench cars. Electric operation. Opened 1991.

BRIDGENORTH, CASTLE HILL FUNICULAR;
The only urban funicular in the UK, links High Town and Low Town. Upper station is in Castle Hill. Enclosed cars entered through bulkhead doors. Electric operation. Track length 65 metres. Opened 1892.

LYNTON AND LYNMOUTH CLIFF RAILWAY; Running from the Esplanade, Lynmouth to Lynton, the railway climbs over 150 metres. Enclosed cars on triangular frames. Hydraulic power. Track length 270 metres. Opened 1890.

Cliff Railways may also be found at:

BOURNEMOUTH, Dorset (3)

BROADSTAIRS, Kent.

FOLKESTONE, Kent.

HASTINGS, Sussex.

SALTBURN, Cleveland.

SCARBOROUGH, Yorkshire. (4)

SOUTHEND, Essex.

Above: The Castle Hill funicular at Bridgenorth, Shropshire.

Bottom Left: Cliff railway at Bournemouth's West Cliff.

Below: The hydraulically powered cliff railway connecting Lynton and Lynmouth in Devon.

APPENDIX 3.

Principal Operating Museums in the Mainland United Kingdom.

BLACK COUNTRY MUSEUM.
Tipton Road, Dudley, W.Midlands.   3' 6" gauge line links the museum entrance with the village area including one intermediate stop. Vehicles are restored cars from the local area.

BRADFORD INDUSTRIAL MUSEUM.
Moorside Mills, Moorside Road, Eccleshill, Bradford, Yorks. Short, standard gauge line operating horse-drawn trams.

CONWY VALLEY RAILWAY MUSEUM.
Old Goods Yard, Betws-y-Coed, Gwynedd.   15" gauge line operating rides within the museum grounds. The car is a purpose-built, eight-wheeled, semi-open single decker.

EAST ANGLIA MUSEUM OF TRANSPORT.
Chapel Road, Carlton Colville, Lowestoft, Suffolk.
Standard gauge line offering 'out and back' rides within the museum complex. Cars from a number of systems within the UK including Blackpool and London as well as Lowestoft. Also operates a four-wheel, single decker car from Amsterdam.

NATIONAL TRAMWAY MUSEUM.
Crich, Matlock, Derbyshire, DE4 5DP.   Standard gauge offering 'out and back' service as well as linking the car park and entrance with the exhibition areas. The museum houses the premier collection in the UK with around sixty cars, many of which are operated on the museum line. The range includes horse, steam and electrically powered vehicles. In addition there are enclosed displays on the development of trams, systems and electricity with full-size tableau including a reconstruction of a 'turn of the century' tramway exhibition. Plans include the provision of displays concerning modern developments.

NORTH OF ENGLAND OPEN AIR MUSEUMS.
Beamish, County Durham. Standard gauge, circular line serving the various areas of the site and linking them with the museum entrance. A range of vehicles is in use, mainly from the north of England.

3'6" gauge line at the Black Country Museum, Dudley, West Midlands.

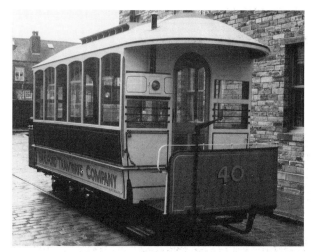

Horse drawn tram at Bradford Industrial Museum.

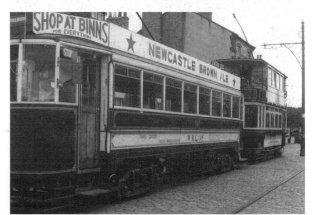

Above:
Trams at Town End, the National Tramway Museum, Crich, Derbyshire.

Top Right:
Purpose built car operating within the grounds at Conwy Valley Railway Museum, Betws-y-Coed, Gwynedd.

Centre Right:
Tram and trolleybus at the East Anglia Museum of Transport, Carlton Colville, near Lowestoft.

Bottom Right:
North of England Open Air Museum, Beamish, County Durham.

SUMMERLEE HERITAGE MUSEUM.
West Canal Street, Coatbridge, Strathclyde. Standard gauge line runs from close to the museum entrance to the reconstructed industrial village. The majority of cars are from continental sources.

TRANSPERIENCE.
Low Moor, Bradford, Yorks. Standard gauge operating within Transperience. Continental and UK vehicles.

WOODSIDE TRAMWAY.
Woodside Ferry Terminal, Birkenhead, Wirral. Standard gauge line linking a number of historic sites in Birkenhead. Presently operating Hong Kong built cars, it is intended to eventually use replicas of local vehicles.

Theme Park Systems.

ALTON TOWERS.
Straddle-type monorail by AEG (Von Roll). Links car park with areas of the theme park.

NATIONAL MOTOR MUSEUM, BEAULIEU, HANTS.
Straddle-type monorail around a closed circuit track. One station. A 'ride' in it's own right rather than a transit system within the complex.

CENTRE FOR ALTERNATIVE TECHNOLOGY, MACHYNLLETH, POWYS.
Hydraulic powered funicular built in 1994. Links car park and entrance with upper part of centre.

Top: Summerlee Heritage Museum, Strathclyde.

Above: Hydraulic powered funicular at the Centre for Alternative Technology, Machynlleth, Powys.

Left: Monorail at Beaulieu, Hampshire.

Non-operating Museums and the Restoration Movement.

In addition to those museums operating trams there are around twenty-five others with trams on static display. Major collections may be found at:

GLASGOW,   Museum of Transport,
Kelvin Hall.

HULL,   Museum of Transport,
High Street.

LONDON,   London Transport Museum,
Covent Garden.
Science Museum,
South Kensington (and at
Wroughton, Wiltshire).

SOUTHEND, Pier Museum.

SWANSEA,   Maritime and Industrial Museum.

As well as vehicles restored for display there are a number which have been restored by private individuals and groups. Many of these are now on display and the movement continues to thrive. Because it is a progressive activity it is not practical to list all private restoration projects. The following examples provide a flavour:

Tram 57 Project, Southampton. Restoring Southampton cars 11 and 38 and looking after Portsmouth car 84.

Conwy Valley. The restoration of Northampton 21 now proceeds elsewhere but its place has been taken by another vehicle. A 1949 Southend Pier car is undergoing restoration at the same site. The site is operated by the Llandudno and Colwyn Bay Electric Railway Society.

Seaton and District Electric Tramway has acquired Exeter 19 from the West of England Transport at Winkleigh and is rebuilding it for operation.

Glasgow Museum of Transport.

Tram 57 Project, Southampton.

Above: Northampton car being restored in the Conwy Valley under the watchful eye of Bronwyn.

Top Right: Preserved tram tracks in Rugby Road, Portsmouth.

Right: There are also preservation and restoration groups for road vehicles. Buses at the West of England Transport Collection, Winkleigh, Devon.

APPENDIX 4.

Guided Transit Systems Planned.

A large number of light rail and other urban transit schemes have been mooted since the early 1980s. Many of these have proved impractical on either political or financial grounds. At the end of 1995 the following projects were at various stages between proposal and the commencement of construction. In some cases where Parliamentary approval has been received, progress has been held up by changing criteria for grant allocation.

AVON, WESTWAY. 34 kilometre, light rail. Initial route between Bradley Stoke and a loop to the south of Bristol city centre. Network extensions planned for later date. Route evaluation in progress. Consultation, enquiries and construction planned before 2000.

CROYDON, TRAMLINK. 28 kilometre, light rail. Network connecting Beckenham, Elmers End, New Addington and Wimbledon via central Croydon. Act of Parliament received Royal Assent 1994. Tendering to design, build and operate began 1995. Work commenced in 1996 with operation anticipated by 2000.

LEEDS, SUPERTRAM. 18 kilometre, light rail. Initial line will link Tingley with the city centre and be extended to Headingley. Further extension is planned for East Leeds. Parliamentary approval received 1993. Tendering process for construction and operation in progress.

MEDWAY METRO. Proposal to link Chatharn and Maidstone with extensions to Gillingham and Kings Hill. Initial consultation commenced 1995. Light rail preferred.

MIDLAND METRO. 78 kilometre, light rail network. Line 1 (20 km. Wolverhampton to Birmingham city centre) achieved Parliamentary consent 1989, the construction consortium (John Laing Plc. and Ansaldo Transporti Spa) was approved 1993 and work commenced 1995. Completion anticipated before 2000.

NOTTINGHAM RAPID TRANSIT. 14 kilometre, light rail. Initial line to link Hucknall with Nottingham city centre. Over half the distance will be on track shared with existing railway. Network extensions planned. Parliamentary approval received 1994. Tendering process is in progress. Operation, originally hoped for by 1998, is now proposed by 2000.

SOUTH EAST HAMPSHIRE RAPID TRANSIT.
Proposed 14 kilometre, light rail line linking Fareham with central Portsmouth, the line will be carried in tunnel under Portsmouth harbour between Gosport and Portsea. Much of the route will use the right of way of the defunct railway between Fareham and Gosport. Guided buses and GLT were considered in earlier stages of consultation. Anticipated operation by early next century.

SEVERN VALE LIGHT RAIL. Proposal to link Gloucester with Cheltenham and their surrounding areas with a gradually extending light rail system. Initial consultation commenced 1994.

GLOSSARY

Articulated. Jointed to allow large cars to negotiate sharp curves. Articulated cars may have from two to five sections mounted, usually, on one more truck than there are sections.

Bogie. Pivoted truck on which the wheels are mounted beneath a tramway or railway vehicle.

Bow Collector. Roof-mounted, sprung frame carrying carbon insert on its top section to collect power from the overhead conductor wire.

Cardan Shaft. Drive shaft with a universal joint at one or both ends, enabling it to drive when the motor and wheels are out of alignment.

Collection Shoe. Conductive 'skate' which runs on the surface of the conductor rail to collect power in 3 and 4 rail systems.

Conductor. (1) Wire or rail which conducts power from the generator to the vehicle.
(2) Individual who acts as guard / time-keeper / fare collector on a passenger transport vehicle.

Conduit Pick-up. Open-topped tube, mounted below ground level between the rails, containing conductor strips on which the collection shoe runs. An early system largely replaced by overhead collection.

Corridor. Access routes to urban centres and heavily-used routes between areas within a city.

Deregulation. The event and effects of removing regulation regarding routes, timetables, fares etc. from road based transport.

Flywheel. Rotating wheel which, when made to spin, effectively stores kinetic energy. This energy may then be transferred to drive a vehicle. The best known examples are in car engines to maintain momentum between power strokes to the crankshaft, in gyroscopes and in 'push and go' toys.

Frequency. The number of vehicles passing a stop in any given time period (e.g. six per hour).

Funicular. Cable-hauled railway, usually on a steep slope, where the cars are permanently attached to the cable and partially counterbalance each other.

Guided Transport. Public transport systems relying on rails, guideways or other form of track to provide automatic steering.

Headway. The period between vehicles passing a stop (e.g. every ten minutes).

Infrastructure. The permanent parts of the system, such as rails, overhead, generators, maintenance facilities etc. which enable the vehicles to carry out their task.

Light Rail. Rail-guided passenger transport system utilising steel wheels on steel rails, often operated by 'line of sight' rules (as opposed to signals) and capable of operating in close proximity with other forms of transport in streets, pedestrian areas and so on. The light relates to passenger capacity and infrastructure compared with conventional railways.

Modular. Construction system in which components are designed to be interchangeable or where they may be used to provide a number of different finished products. An example would be light rail vehicles which could be constructed with varying numbers of sections, driving wheels, either be single or double ended using the same basic range of components.

Monocoque. Form of construction in which the main strength of the structure comes from its shell and shape rather than an internal framework.

Overhead. The conductor wire and its supports.

Pantograph. A flexible framework on top of a vehicle designed to pick up current from the overhead. The collector strip always retains the same position relative to the top of the car regardless of how far up the pantograph is extended.

Pavoir. Brick, concrete or stone slab used for street surface finishing.

Profile, Rail. The shape of the section of a rail, in particular the part which is in contact with the wheel.

Profile, Wheel. The shape of the section of the running surface of the wheel, i.e. that part in contact with the rail.

Rheostat. A form of variable resistance built into an electrical circuit to enable the power to be controlled.

Setts. Stone, concrete, brick or, occasionally, wooden blocks used to fill in the area between and alongside the rails. May be used to demarcate the area 'swept' by the vehicle.

Stringers. Part of a vehicle frame which run along the length of the structure.

Trolley. **(1)** The wheel (or carbon block) at the outer end of the pick-up pole which actually makes contact with the wire and collects the current.
(2) American term for tram, as is 'streetcar'.

Trolley Head. The frame on which the trolley is mounted. It may be either fixed (relative to the trolley-pole) or swivelling to enable the wheel or block to negotiate changes in the direction of the wire.

Truck. Frame mounted below the car carrying the wheels, motor, brakes and ancillary systems.

Select Bibliography.

Abbott J.	'Docklands Light Railway'	London	1991
Abdo J.	'Tram Tours of Lisbon'	Lisbon	1991
Abell P. H.	'British Tramway Guide (4th. Edition)'	Leicester	1993
Alvin J. et al	'Petite Histoire des Transportes en Commun a Bruxelles'	Brussels	1993
Alvin J.	'Vehicules de la STIB'	Brussels	1994
Anderson R.	'Great Orme Tramway, The First 80 Years'	Broxbourn	(No date)
Anon	'Amberley Museum' - Guide	Norwich	1993
Anon	'East Anglia Transport Museum' - Guide	Norwich	1986
Anon	'Lynton and Lynmouth Cliff Railway'	Lynmouth	(No date)
Anon	'National Tramway Museum' - Guide	Crich	1992
Anon	'The Blackpool Tramway'	Crich	1981
ATAC	'Una Corsa Nel Passato - Mostra Retrospettiva Fotografica'	Rome	1990
Baptista A. & J. Lagrange	'O Livro da Carris'	Lisbon	1993
Barnabe G.	'The Railways & Tramways of Majorca'	Brighton	1993
Bateman D. L.	'Tracks to the Cities'		1994
Bayman B. & P. Connor	'Underground, Official Handbook'	London	1994
Buckley R.	'Trams in German Speaking Countries'	Sheffield	1977
Buckley R.	'Tramways and Light Railways of Switzerland and Austria'	Milton Keynes	1984
Bus & Coach Council	'The Future of the Bus'	London	1982
Bushell C.	'Janes Urban Transport Systems 1992 - 3'	Coulsdon	1992
Chalk D, L,	'Bournemouth Transport, 75 Years'	Bournemouth	1977
Chalk D. L.	'Yellow Buses, 85th. Anniversary'	Bournemouth	1987
Cristensen W.	'Historien om Linie 5'	Copenhagen	1976
Christy G. (Ed.)	'Black Country Museum' - Guide		1991
Clayton P. G.	'The Iron Road to Soller'	Brentford	1992
Commission of the European Communities DG111	'Key Factors for the Development of European Urban Guided Transit Suppliers, Final Report & Appendicies'		1993
Commission of the European Communities Directorate-General for Energy DG XVII	'Energy and Environmental Implications of Light Rail Systems'	Harwell	1994

CPPTD	'Portsmouth - 75 Years of Transport'	Portsmouth	1973
Dean I.	'Industrial Narrow Gauge Railways'	Princes Risborough	1985
Ellis N.	'Trams on Old Picture Postcards'	Nottingham	1986
Fox P. et al	'Tram to Supertram'	Sheffield	1995
Frost K. & D. Carson	'Southend Pier Railway'	Romford	1990
Garbutt P.	'World Metro Systems'	London	1989
Goodwyn A.	'Snaefell Mountain Railway'	Douglas	1987
Gwylt C. F.	'A History of the Castle Hill Railway'	Bridgenorth	(No date)
Harris D. et al	'Beamish - A Brief Guide'	Beamish	(No date)
Helin M.	'Han-sur-Lesse - Le Tram des Grottes'	Rhode St. Genese	1982
Holt. D.	'Manchester Metrolink'	Sheffield	1992
Horne J. B.	'One Hundred Years of Southampton Transport'	Southampton	1979
Hostettler E. (Ed.)	'Travelling Light'	London	1987
Hyde D. L.	'Blackpool's New Tramcars'	Crich	1985
Jackson A.	'Volk's Railways, Brighton - An Illustrated History'	Brighton	1993
Jackson C. (Ed.)	'Developing Metros'	Sutton	1995
Johnson P.	'British Trams & Tramways in the 1980s'	London	1985
Johnson P.	'Trams in Blackpool'	Leicester	1986
Johnson P.	'The Welsh Narrow Gauge Railways'	London	1991
Joyce J.	'Blackpool's Trams'	London	1985
King V. & J.Price	'The Tramways of Portugal'	Broxbourne	1983
Kirby A.	'Heaton Park & Its Transport'	Manchester	1981
Kirby A.	'Manchester's Little Tram'	Manchester	1990
Leicester Museum Service	'Brush Electric Street Cars (Catalogue 1912)	Leicester	1980
Ogden E. & J. Senior	'Metrolink, Official Handbook'	Glossop	1991
Orchard A.	'Blackpool North Pier Tramway'	Blackpool	(No date)
Parry Peoplemovers	'A Light Tramway for Brighton'	Cradley Heath	(No date)
Passenger Transport Executive Group	'Light Rail Transit'		1988
Pearce A. et al	'Docklands Light Railway, Official Handbook'	London	1994
Price J.	'Seaton Tramway'	Seaton	(No date)
Price J. et al	'Tramways & Light Railways of Austria, Hungary & Yugoslavia'	Berlin / London	1988
Price J. & J. Wyse (Trans.)	'Tramway & Light Railway Atlas, Germany, 1992'	Berlin / London	1993

PTRC	'Public Transport Planning & Operations - Report of the 17th. Summer Annual Meeting'	Brighton	1989
Pulling J.	'Volk's Railway, Brighton - Centenary'	Brighton	1983
Quetelard B. et al	'Six Ans de Metro dans la Communaute Urbaine de Lille'	Lille	1988
Redecker A. & J. Whitelegg	'A Clean Environment & A Sound Economy; European Transport Solutions for Lancaster & Morecombe'	Lancaster	1992
Richards B.	'Transport in Cities'	London	1990
San Francisco Municipal Railway	'Short Range Transit Plan & Capital Improvement Program, 1993 - 2002'	San Francisco	1993
Sebree M. et al (Eds.)	'North American Light Rail Annual & Users' Guide for 1992'	Glendale	1991
Sebree M. et al (Eds.)	'North American Light Rail Annual & Users' Guide for 1993'	Glendale	1992
Smith A. & N. Smith	'Restoration of Southampton Trams 11, 38 & 57'	Southampton	(No date)
Smith P.	'Llandudno & Colwyn Bay Electric Railway in the 1920s'	Conwy	(No date)
Smith P.	'By Tram to the Summit'	Colwyn Bay	1983
Stadtwerke-Munchen Verkehrsbetriebe	'100 Jahre Munchner Trambahn'	Munich	1976
Stewart I.	'Tramway Museum Stock Book'	Crich	1992
Taplin M.	'Light Rail Transit Today'	Milton Keynes	(No date)
Taplin M.	'Tramways of Eastern Germany'	London	1972
Taplin M.	'Tramways of Western Germany'	London	1973
Taplin M.	'Light Rail in Europe'	London	1995
Taplin M. & P. Fox (Eds.)	'Light Railway Review 1 - 7' (Annual)	Sheffield	1990 - 1996
Turner K.	'Old Trams'	Princes Risborough	1985
Villa S.	'Senni di Storia Aziendale'	Rome	1990
Waller P. (Ed.)	'Supertram'	London	1990
Wangemann V.	'Berlin Public Transport'	Chelmsford	1984
Viener Stadtwerke-Verkehrsbetriebe	'Die Entwicklung Des Offenlichen Verkehrs In Wien'	Vienna	1987
Winston Bond A.	'The British Tram, History's Orphan'		1980
Woodhams J.	'Funicular Railways'	Princes Risborough	1989

DLR OPENED 1987

BANK EXTENSION 1991

BECKTON EXTENSION 1994

LATE EVENING AND
WEEKEND SERVICES 1994/5

NEW FLEET OF TRAINS 1995

NEW CONTROL SYSTEM 1996

MORE FREQUENT SERVICES 1997/8

MILLENNIUM CABLE CAR 1999

LEWISHAM EXTENSION 2000

FUTURE DEVELOPMENTS ....2000+

The
way
ahead

DOCKLANDS
LIGHT RAIL ®

Cover illustration and above: Eurotram, Strasbourg
ABB Daimler-Benz Transportation Rolling Stock
Litchurch Lane
Derby DE24 8AD
Tel: +44 1332 344666
Fax: +44 1332 266289